The Biblical Psalms
in Christian Worship

The CALVIN INSTITUTE OF CHRISTIAN WORSHIP LITURGICAL STUDIES Series, edited by John D. Witvliet, is designed to promote reflection on the history, theology, and practice of Christian worship and to stimulate worship renewal in Christian congregations. Contributions include writings by pastoral worship leaders from a wide range of communities and scholars from a wide range of disciplines. The ultimate goal of these contributions is to nurture worship practices that are spiritually vital and theologically rooted.

PUBLISHED

Gather into One: Praying and Singing Globally
C. Michael Hawn

The Substance of Things Seen: Art, Faith, and the Christian Community
Robin M. Jensen

Wonderful Words of Life:
Hymns in American Protestant History and Theology
Richard J. Mouw and Mark A. Noll, Editors

Discerning the Spirits:
A Guide to Thinking about Christian Worship Today
Cornelius Plantinga Jr. and Sue A. Rozeboom

Voicing God's Psalms
Calvin Seerveld

My Only Comfort: Death, Deliverance, and Discipleship
in the Music of Bach
Calvin R. Stapert

The Biblical Psalms in Christian Worship

A BRIEF INTRODUCTION AND
GUIDE TO RESOURCES

John D. Witvliet

William B. Eerdmans Publishing Company

Grand Rapids, Michigan / Cambridge, U.K.

Published 2007 by
Wm. B. Eerdmans Publishing Co.
2140 Oak Industrial Drive N.E., Grand Rapids, Michigan 49505 /
P.O. Box 163, Cambridge CB3 9PU U.K.

Printed in the United States of America

11 10 09 08 07   7 6 5 4 3 2 1

ISBN 978-0-8028-0767-0

LCNN: 2006039057
169 p; 24 cm
BS1435 W58   2007

www.eerdmans.com

Dedicated to

Sheila Grace, Katherine, Madeline, and Luke

May God's Spirit grace you with a lifetime of praying the Psalms

(Ps. 145:4)

Contents

Preface

This brief book arises out of three observations.

First, the Psalms are a font of inspiration, encouragement, and instruction in the life of both public and private prayer. From Basil to Bonhoeffer to Bono, the enthusiasm that emanates from wise Christian writers of every historical period points to the Psalms as one of the richest sources of wisdom for the practice of worship. The historical testimonies found throughout this volume are a compelling call to recover the practice of praying the Psalms.

Second, there is relatively tepid enthusiasm for the Psalms in worship throughout vast stretches of North American Christianity. This is the bad news. Indeed, as I visit congregations and worship conferences across the spectrum of denominations, I often find enthusiasm for a particular musical or dramatic setting of a Psalm, but relatively little interest in a sustained attempt to pray the Psalms over time (though there are notable exceptions). Many churches do use lectionary-based Psalms each week, but often they are rendered without enthusiasm or understanding.

Most often, those who dismiss the Psalms associate them with music they don't like, usually by mistakenly assuming that Psalmody necessarily entails either overly sumptuous Victorian choral harmonies, dirge-like chorales, sentimental folk music, or inaccessible chant. The good news is that this volume can catalog hundreds of worship resources in many spoken, musical, and visual idioms — so much so that nearly everyone will find resources here they will both love and hate. The last thirty years has witnessed an outpouring of creativity. The problem is that these resources are not often used in a consistent way that encourages deep participation in worship. We live in a time of both need and opportunity in the practice of worship, but particularly with respect to the role of the Psalms in worship.

Third, we have unprecedented access to vast amounts of information about the Psalms, as well as copious resources for using them in worship. Taking into account all commentaries, introductions, devotionals, musical settings, educational curricula, and historical studies, there are now over 3,000 volumes on the Psalms in print, in addition to thousands of websites. One goal of this book is to provide an orientation to this material. The quality of a good deal of this material is heartening. The challenge is putting this material to good use for the sake of the church.

1. Aims and Audience

In light of these observations, this book is designed to be a catalyst for a renewed engagement with the Psalms in the context of public worship. My overarching goal is both to promote and to discipline the creativity we bring to praying the Psalms in community. With this goal in mind, I do not aim to provide a summary of all possible themes related to the Psalms, but rather to highlight those themes that bear especially on their use in worship. Specifically, I gather up insights from and provide some orientation to four bodies of literature that are often disconnected from each other:

- biblical scholarship on the Old Testament and Hebrew Bible;
- writings on the history, theology, and pastoral practice of worship, liturgy, and preaching;
- writings on the history and practice of church music; and
- currently available liturgical and musical resources.

Given the complexity of each body of material, I am very aware of how difficult it is to present a fair and balanced account of each, especially in a relatively brief publication. I already look forward to opportunities to revise this material in light of reader feedback and new and emerging resources that will be published in the next few years.

My primary intended audience consists of people who would be drawn to at least one of these four bodies of literature. The audience includes:

- students in courses in Old Testament/Hebrew Bible, liturgy or worship, preaching, and church music (my hope is that this is a brief enough volume to function as a supplemental text in any of these courses — and preferably, within a seminary, divinity school, or church-related college, it could be used in courses in each of these areas);
- practitioners in local congregations, including pastors, preachers, musicians, artists, worship planners and leaders, and church educators;
- scholars and teachers in one of these four areas, particularly among those looking for an orientation to the other fields;
- songwriters, artists, dramatists, hymnal and resource development committees, and publishers looking for access to a wide range of available resources and for strategies to help congregations pray the Psalms;
- librarians (one good place for all readers to begin with this book is by talking with your school or congregational librarian about the resources described here; relatively few libraries have strong holdings in each of the four literatures cataloged here).

Each of these audiences tends to read quite different books on the Psalms and to approach the Psalms in quite different ways. This volume offers some cross training to each group. With these multiple audiences, each reader will likely find some sections that are of more interest than others. My hope is that each reader might discover some helpful insights from literature they might not normally read. This can be a "passageway book"; it will be well used if it leads readers to other fine sources.

Also, I have set aside the normal aversion to footnotes in short introductory volumes. My intention is for the footnotes to serve as a guide to further research. Students who want to explore a topic found here could begin by studying noted material. The bibliography at the end of the volume is supplemental to the footnotes. I realize that producing a compressed digest of all this material makes the book a bit less lyrical than I might have liked. But if it leads readers to some of the wonderful scholarly, devotional, and artistic materials cited in the notes, it will have been worth the sacrifice.

Part of this more lyrical voice is also supplied by the interludes from major historical studies of the Psalms. Every one of these quotations qualifies as an "encomium," an expression of high praise. In preparing this material, I was struck time and time again by how so many of the most significant pastoral and theological figures in the history of the church reserved some of their most glowing words of gratitude for the Psalms. This material not only introduces a rhapsodic tone to the book, but may also offer some quotable epigrams for course syllabi, congregational newsletters — or e-mail signatures!

2. ECUMENICAL AUDIENCE

I am also attempting to write this volume with an awareness of a broad ecumenical range of practices, including lectionary-based Psalmody in Roman Catholic, Anglican, Lutheran, Methodist, and Presbyterian sources, Presbyterian and Reformed metrical Psalmody, and the growing use of the Psalter in evangelical, Pentecostal, Charismatic and emerging worship traditions. Our work at the Calvin Institute of Christian Worship addresses congregations in nearly every Christian tradition. We aim to do so with strong confessional convictions shaped by our Reformed identity, but also with an eagerness to be in conversation with Christians in many traditions.

I begin with a vivid awareness of what radically different practices come to mind when readers across this spectrum of Christianity think about the Psalms in worship. Some readers will come from churches whose liturgy and music is quite fixed, liturgical, and well-established. Churches in this group frequently limit their use of Psalmody to Psalms recommended by the lectionary and limit their mode of rendering the Psalms to the published offerings of a favorite musical publisher. I hope that this material will help readers from these traditions to new appreciation for historic practices, as well as to questions that may suggest liturgical improvisations that will enhance and deepen participation.

Other readers will come from congregations that pour enormous resources into creative worship expressions, generating new songs, dramatic scripts, video clips, and other elements of worship on a regular basis. I hope that readers from these congregations will reconsider the ancient Psalms as one of the most trustworthy sources and models for creativity in worship.

Perhaps the majority of readers will come from congregations with limited resources for worship, in terms of preparation time, musical or artistic talent, and collaborative planning processes. My hope is that these readers will discover here a resource or a way of rendering the Psalms that is at once accessible and appropriately challenging for their particular congregation.

It has also occurred to me that nearly every reader will find some of what follows to be a bit perplexing. Preachers who do not use, or are not aware of, the lectionary may not realize its value for their use. Lectionary users may not realize how large a portion of the Psalms they are missing in worship. Congregations who chant Psalms do not often read material about praise choruses. Emerging church leaders may not be aware of the outpouring of recent music in multiple musical styles for responsorial psalmody. Congregations with quite formal worship may not have considered using a speech choir alongside of an "anthem choir." Congregations with informal worship may not have considered the value of analytic study of the Psalms prior to their use in worship. All of this means that readers will use this material in remarkably different ways, depending on where they find themselves in the broad Christian landscape.

The breadth of the intended audience has led me to a different approach from some volumes on this subject. Earlier volumes on the Psalms in worship, such as those by J. A. Lamb and Massey H. Shepherd Jr., addressed an audience of Roman Catholic, Lutheran, Anglican, Methodist, and Reformed congregations, and primarily outlined the history of liturgical development in the West. My audience includes these traditions, but also includes congregations known variously as evangelical, free church, low-church, contemporary and/or emerging. In this context, a more topical approach seemed a wiser route, with historical examples interspersed occasionally throughout.

There are also inevitable limitations to the ecumenical scope of any volume. For example, this volume does not address in detail the role of Psalmody in Orthodox worship, in monastic worship, in worship in the global South and East. Perhaps there will be occasion to develop a second edition that more fully engages with these parts of the body of Christ.

Further, this book focuses primarily on a congregation's weekly assembly for worship. I acknowledge and celebrate the tradition of daily public prayer that has provided the most regular setting for psalmody in many Christian traditions. I am eager to promote the recovery of public daily prayer, with copious Psalm singing.[1] But for the majority of congregations in North America, the primary focus for worship renewal remains the weekly (usually Sunday) assembly of the church.

This ecumenical approach has some downsides. The limited space in this brief book does not allow me to speak to the specifics of the liturgical use of the Psalms in any particular tradition — a Reformed or Methodist Lord's Supper service, for example, or a Pentecostal prayer meeting, or a Catholic morning prayer service. It also does not provide me with the best context to speak in a sustained way about inclusive language translations. The nuances of that discussion across Catholic, Protestant, and Pentecostal communities are so complex that they could easily occupy a full volume on their own.

But this ecumenical approach also has some decided advantages. Over and over again, I have been struck by how the Psalms encompass both sides of some of the most striking divisions within Christian communities today. The Psalms speak of both social justice and personal transformation; they embody hand-clapping exuberance and profound introspection; they express the prayers of both the exalted and the lowly; they are fully alive in the present, but always point to the future on the basis of the past; they highlight both the extravagance of grace and the joy of faithful obedience; they express a restless yearning for change and a profound gratitude for the inheritance of faith; they protest ritualism but embody the richest expression of ritual prayer. It's little wonder, then, that any journey into literature on the Psalms will quite quickly lead us to materials produced by neo-Puritan Calvinists, Catholic mystics, social justice activists, and charismatic worship leaders. (Perhaps some of these groups can encounter each other through this book!)

1. See, for example, Dorothy C. Bass, *Receiving the Day: Christian Practices for Opening the Gift of Time* (San Francisco: Jossey-Bass, 2000), pp. 22-24; Arthur Paul Boers, *The Rhythm of God's Grace: Uncovering Morning and Evening Hours of Prayer* (Brewster, MA: Paraclete Press, 2003); Gregory W. Woolfenden, *Daily Liturgical Prayer: Origins and Theology* (Aldershot: Ashgate, 2004); Paul F. Bradshaw, *Two Ways of Praying* (Nashville: Abingdon Press, 1995).

This breadth can lead each tradition or group within the broad church to latch on to only the portions of the Psalms that match its theological emphases or preferred type of piety. At the same time, the good news is that the Psalms give each community and each believer an opportunity to work their weak sides, to develop habits and modes of prayer that do not come naturally.

Indeed, may God's Spirit use this work to help us all work our weak sides, and to grow in us a deeper faith and more robust public prayer.

The Biblical Psalms
in Christian Worship

Patristic Testimonies

Basil (c. 330-379)   All Scripture is inspired by God for our benefit; it was composed by the Spirit for this reason, that all we men, as if at a common surgery for souls, might each of us select a remedy for his particular malady. 'Care', it is said, 'makes the greatest sin to cease'. Now the Prophets teach certain things, the Historians and the Law teach others, and Proverbs provides still a different sort of advice, but the Book of Psalms encompasses the benefit of them all. It foretells what is to come and memorializes history; it legislates for life, gives advice on practical matters, and serves in general as a repository of good teachings, carefully searching out what is suitable for each individual.

What did the Holy Spirit do when he saw that the human race was not led easily to virtue, and that due to our penchant for pleasure we gave little heed to an upright life? He mixed sweetness of melody with doctrine so that inadvertently we would absorb the benefit of the words through gentleness and ease of hearing, just as clever physicians frequently smear the cup with honey when giving the fastidious some rather bitter medicine to drink. Thus he contrived for us these harmonious psalm tunes, so that those who are children in actual age as well as those who are young in behavior, while appearing only to sing would in reality be training their souls. For not one of these many indifferent people ever leaves church easily retaining in memory some maxim of either the Apostles or the Prophets, but they do sing the texts of the Psalms at home and circulate them in the marketplace.

A Psalm is tranquility of soul and the arbitration of peace; it settles one's tumultuous and seething thoughts. It mollifies the soul's wrath and chastens its recalcitrance. A psalm creates friendships, unites the separated and reconciles those at enmity. Who can still consider one to be a foe with whom one utters the same prayer to God! Thus psalmody provides the greatest of all goods, charity, by devising in its common song a certain bond of unity, and by joining together the people into the concord of a single chorus.

Basil the Great, *Homilia in psalmum i; Patrologiae cursus completus, series graeca*, ed. J. P. Migne (Paris, 1960), vol. XXIX, pp. 209-12; trans. in James McKinnon, *Music in Early Christian Literature* (New York: Cambridge University Press, 1987), p. 65

Ambrose (c. 339-397) History teaches, the Law instructs, prophecy proclaims, reproach chastens and moralizing persuades; in the Book of Psalms there is the successful accomplishment of all this along with a kind of balm of human salvation. Whoever reads there, has a special remedy whereby he can cure the wounds of selfish passion. Whoever is willing to look closely, discovers a variety of contests prepared for him, as if in a communal gymnasium of souls or a stadium of virtue, from which he can select for himself the one for which he knows himself best suited, in which he can more easily win the crown. If one is eager to study the deeds of our forebears and wishes to imitate them, he finds contained within a single psalm the entire range of ancestral history so that he gains a treasury of memories as a stipend for his reading. Things explained with more brevity also seem easier.

What is more pleasing than a psalm? David himself puts it nicely: 'Praise the Lord', he says, 'for a psalm is good' (Ps. 146.1). And indeed! A psalm is the blessing of the people, the praise of God, the commendation of the multitude, the applause of all, the speech of every man, the voice of the Church, the sonorous profession of faith, devotion full of authority, the joy of liberty, the noise of good cheer, and the echo of gladness. It softens anger, it gives release from anxiety, it alleviates sorrow; it is protection at night, instruction by day, a shield in time of fear, a feast of holiness, the image of tranquility, a pledge of peace and harmony, which produces one song from various and sundry voices in the manner of a cithara. The day's dawning resounds with a psalm, with a psalm its passing echoes.

The Apostle admonishes women to be silent in church, yet they do well to join in a psalm; this is gratifying for all ages and fitting for both sexes. Old men ignore the stiffness of age to sing [a psalm], and melancholy veterans echo it in the joy of their hearts; young men sing one without the bane of lust, as do adolescents without threat from their insecure age or the temptation of sensual pleasure; even young women sing psalms with no loss of wifely decency, and girls sing a hymn to God with sweet and supple voice while maintaining decorum and suffering no lapse of modesty. Youth is eager to understand [a psalm], and the child who refuses to learn other things takes pleasure in contemplating it; it is a kind of play, productive of more learning than that which is dispensed with stern discipline. With what great effort is silence maintained in church during the readings *(cum lections leguntur)!* If just one person recites, the entire congregation makes noise; but when a psalm is read *(legitur),* it is itself the guarantor of silence because when all speak [in the response] no one makes noise. Kings put aside the arrogance of power and sing a psalm, as David himself was glad to be observed in this function; a psalm, then, is sung by emperors and rejoiced in by the people. Individuals vie in proclaiming what is of profit to all. A psalm is sung at home and repeated outdoors; it is learned without effort and retained with delight. A psalm joins those with differences, unites those at odds and reconciles those who have been offended, for who will not concede to him with whom one sings to God in one voice? It is after all a great bond of unity for the full number of people to join in one chorus. The strings of the cithara differ, but create one harmony *(symphonia).* The fingers of a musician *(artificis)* often go astray among the strings though they are very few in number, but among the people the Spirit musician knows not how to err.

Ambrose, *Explanatio psalmi i, 9; Patrologiae cursus completus, series latina,* ed. J. P. Migne (Paris, 1960), vol. XIV, pp. 924-25; trans. in James McKinnon, *Music in Early Christian Literature* (New York: Cambridge University Press, 1987), p. 126

John Chrysostom (c. 347-407)

Since this sort of pleasure is natural to our soul, and lest the demons introduce licentious songs and upset everything, God erected the barrier of the psalms, so that they would be a matter of both pleasure and profit. For from strange songs, harm and destruction enter in along with many a dread thing, since what is wanton and contrary to the law in these songs settles in the various parts of the soul, rendering it weak and soft. But from the spiritual psalms can come considerable pleasure, much that is useful, much that is holy, and the foundation of all philosophy, as these texts cleanse the soul and the Holy Spirit flies swiftly to the soul who sings such songs.

I say these things, not so that you alone sing praise, but so that you teach your children and wives also to sing such songs, not only while weaving or while engaged in other tasks, but especially at table. For since the devil generally lies in wait at banquets, having as his allies drunkenness and gluttony, along with inordinate laughter and an unbridled spirit, it is necessary especially then, both before and after the meal, to construct a defense against him from the psalms, and to arise from the banquet together with wife and children to sing sacred hymns to God.

And let us stand together and say: 'Thou has made us glad, Lord, in thy work, and in the works of thy hands we will rejoice' (Ps. 91.5). And after the psalmody prayer is to be offered, so that we might also sanctify the house itself along with the soul. Just as those who introduce actors, dancers and prostitutes into banquets, also summon there demons and the devil, and fill their homes with every manner of discord — instances of jealousy, adultery, fornication and numerous other dread things — so those who call upon David with his cithara, call upon Christ inwardly through him. Where Christ is, no demon would dare enter, indeed none would even dare peep in there; rather would peace, love, and all good things flow as from fountains. Those other make a theatre of their house; you must make a church of your home. For where there is a psalm, prayer, the dance (χορεία) of prophets, and a pious attitude among the singers, one would not err in calling such a gathering a church.

John Chrysostom, *In psalmum xli,* 1-2; *Patrologiae cursus completus, series graeca,* ed. J. P. Migne (Paris, 1960), vol. LV, p. 157; trans. in James McKinnon, *Music in Early Christian Literature* (New York: Cambridge University Press, 1987), pp. 80-81

Athanasius (c. 295-373)

And, among all the books, the Psalter has certainly a very special grace, a choiceness of quality well worthy to be pondered; for, besides the characteristics which it shares with others, it has this peculiar marvel of its own, that within it are represented and portrayed in all their great variety the movements of the human soul. It is like a picture, in which you see yourself portrayed and, seeing, may understand and consequently form yourself upon the pattern given. Elsewhere in the Bible you read only that the Law commands this or that to be done, you listen to the Prophets to learn about the Saviour's coming or you turn to the historical books to learn the doings of the kings and holy men; but in the Psalter, besides all these things, you learn about *yourself.* You find depicted in it all the movements of your soul, all its changes, its ups and downs, its failures and recoveries. . . .

. . . For he who reads those books is clearly reading not his own words but those of holy men and other people about whom they write; but the marvel with the Psalter is that, barring those prophecies about the Saviour and some about the Gentiles, the reader takes all its words upon his lips as though they were his own, and each one sings the Psalms as though they had been written for his special benefit, and takes them and recites them, not as though someone else were speaking or another person's feelings being described, but as himself speaking of himself, offering the words to God as his own heart's utterance, just as though he himself had made them up. Not as the words of the patriarchs or of Moses and the other prophets will he reverence these: no, he is bold to take them as his own and written for his very self. Whether he has kept the Law or whether he has broken it, it is his own doings that the Psalms describe; every one is bound to find his very self in them and, be he faithful soul or be he sinner, each reads in them descriptions of himself.

It seems to me, moreover, that because the Psalms thus serve him who sings them as a mirror, wherein he sees himself and his own soul, he cannot help but render them in such a manner that their words go home with equal force to those who hear him sing, and stir them also to a like reaction. Sometimes it is repentance that is generated in this way, as by the conscience-stirring words of Psalm 51; another time, hearing how God helps those who hope and trust in Him, the listener too rejoices and begins to render thanks, as though that gracious help already were his own. Psalm 3, to take another instance, a man will sing, bearing his own afflictions in his mind; Psalms 11 and 12 he will use as the expression of his own faith and prayer; and singing the 54th, the 56th, the 57th, and the 142nd, it is not as though someone else was being persecuted but out of his own experience that he renders praise to God. And every other Psalm is spoken and composed by the Spirit in the selfsame way: just as in a mirror, the movements of our own souls are reflected in them and the words are indeed are very own, given us to serve both as a reminder of our changes of condition and as a pattern and model for the amendment of our lives. . . .

Athanasius, *On the Incarnation* (Crestwood, NY: St. Vladimir's Orthodox Theological Seminary, 1946), pp. 103, 105-6

Niceta of Remesiana (d. after 414)

What do you fail to find in the psalms of David that works toward the benefit, edification and consolation of the human species of whatever class, sex or age? The infant has here what he can suckle, the boy what he can cheer, the adolescent that by which he can mend his ways, the young man what he can follow and the old man material for prayer. A woman learns modesty, orphans find a father, widows a judge, the poor a protector and strangers a guide. Kings and judges hear what they should fear. A psalm consoles the sad, restrains the joyful, tempers the angry, refreshes the poor and chides the rich man to know himself. To absolutely all who will take it, the psalm offers an appropriate medicine; nor does it despise the sinner, but presses upon him the wholesome remedy of penitential tears.

For since human nature rejects and avoids what is difficult, even if beneficial, and accepts virtually nothing unless it seems to offer pleasure, through David the Lord prepares for men this potion which is sweet by reason of its melody *(cantionem)* and effective in the cure of disease by reason of its strength. For a psalm is sweet to the ear when sung, it penetrates the soul when it gives pleasure, it is easily remembered when sung often, and what the harshness of the Law cannot force from the minds of man it excludes by the suavity of song. For whatever the Law, the Prophets and even the Gospels teach is contained as a remedy in the sweetness of these songs.

Niceta of Remesiana, *De utilitate hymnorum* 5, 7; C. Turner, "Niceta of Remesiana II: Introduction and text of 'De psalmodiae bono,'" *Journal of Theological Studies* 24 (1922-23): 235-37; trans. in James McKinnon, *Music in Early Christian Literature* (New York: Cambridge University Press, 1987), pp. 135-36

Cassiodorus (c. 485–c. 580) The psalms make our vigils pleasant when in the silence of night the choirs hymn their praise. The human voice bursts into melody, and with words skilfully set to music it leads us back to Him from whom divine eloquence has come for the salvation of the human race. The united voices of the singers become a song which delights ears and instructs souls. In company with the divine angels whom we cannot hear, we mingle words of praise through Him who came from the seed of David, the Lord Christ. As He Himself says in the Apocalypse: *I am the root and the source of David* [Apocalypse 22.16]. From Him we have both obtained our saving religion and have come to know the revealed mysteries of the holy Trinity. So the psalms rightly unite the undivided glory of Father, Son, and Holy Spirit, so that their praise is proved to be perfect.

Truly they are vessels of truth, for they contain so many virtues, they are suffused with so many odours of heaven, and they are thronged with so many celestial treasures. They are the water-jugs containing the heavenly wine and keeping it ever fresh and undiluted. Their marvelous sweetness does not grow bitter with worldly corruptions, but retains its worth and is continually enhanced with the grace of the purest sweetness. They are a most abundant store, the fecundity of which cannot be exhausted, although so many peoples of the earth drink of it.

What a wondrous sweetness flows from them when sung! When hymned by men's voices they rival the pleasant-sounding organ; when loudly shouted they echo trumpet-sounds; and by the mingling of living chords they produce the sound of the harp. The notes previously observed as issuing from musical instruments are now seen to emanate from the rational bodies of men. But we are not to sing like parrots and larks which seek to imitate men's words but are known to be utterly unaware of what they sing. True, a charming song delights our minds, but does not impel them to fruitful tears; it soothes the ears but does not direct its hearers to heavenly things. But we are pricked at heart if we can heed what our lips can say.

Cassiodorus: Explanation of the Psalms, vol. 1, trans. P. G. Walsh (New York/Mahwah, NJ: Paulist Press, 1990), pp. 24-26

PART I

The Psalms and the Basic Grammar
of Christian Worship

Learning to talk is one of life's greatest miracles. But even for toddlers, healthy speech habits don't come naturally. Young children need to learn to say "thank you," "I'm sorry," and "please." Parents need to prompt and reinforce these basic conversational moves. Eventually they become part of the way toddlers see the world and navigate relationships. Indeed, there are few moments quite as sweet as hearing a sudden, unprompted "Thanks, Mommy and Daddy."

I love you . . . I'm sorry . . . Thank you . . . Help . . . Words like these are the building blocks of healthy relationships. Every close relationship depends on them. When they are left unpracticed, marriages fail and friendships disintegrate.

Faithful speech is also central to the Christian life. One of the most provocative and inspiring word pictures in all of Scripture is that God is related to the church like a marriage partner. The God of the Bible is not just interested in being contemplated or appeased. This God is interested in the give and take of faithful life together, with good communication right at the center of it. Ample evidence for this claim is the Bible's songbook, the 150 Psalms, each of which expresses at least one essential communicational habit for a people in a covenant relationship with God.

One of the ways we learn good communication habits with God is by participating in public worship. When we gather for worship, the church invites us to join together to say to God, "We love you. We're sorry. Come again — we're listening. Help. Thank you. I will serve you." In fact, some orders of worship pretty much follow this pattern, ensuring a healthy balanced diet of faithful speech. To use a phrase from Thomas G. Long's recent book *Testimony,* worship is "God's language school." As Long explains:

> The way we talk in worship affects the way we talk in the rest of our lives, and vice versa. . . . The words of worship are like stones thrown into the pond; they ripple outward in countless concentric circles, finding ever fresh expression in new places in our lives. . . . Worship is a key element in the church's "language school" for life. . . . It's a provocative idea — worship as a soundtrack for the rest of life, the words and music and actions of worship inside the sanctuary playing the background as we live our lives outside, in the world.[1]

As with toddlers, these speech habits take practice. But the discipline is worth it, forming us over time to express our deepest fears, hopes, and joys in profound ways.

The challenge is that on any given Sunday, each of us comes to church with something different to say. Some of us come to church ready to tell God "thank you!" Others of us want to cry "why?" Others are ready to say "I'm sorry" — though we all need to. To say it another way, some of us come ready to sing Psalm 100, others Psalm 13, and all us, if we're honest, need to speak Psalm 51. Good worship services make room for these essential words. They help each of us express our particular experience, but they also help us practice forms of speech we're still growing into. This is one reason public worship is so important — it challenges us to practice forms of faithful speech to God that we are not likely to try on our own. Authentic worship, like toddler talk, expresses who we are and forms what we are becoming.

The biblical Psalms are the foundational mentor and guide in this vocabulary and grammar for worship. In a provocative and inspiring book, Eugene

1. Thomas G. Long, *Testimony: Talking Ourselves into Being Christian* (San Francisco: Jossey-Bass, 2004), pp. 47-48. Long also suggests: "When a congregation every single Sunday of the year sings the psalms, they acquire a vocabulary that touches the raw nerve of every possible human emotion but always come unfailingly around to praise. In doing so, they are worshiping, but they are also in training to know how to speak when out in the world: candidly and honestly, but never cynically or despairingly" (p. 33).

Peterson speaks of the Psalms as the tools God has given us to form in us a vibrant and well-grounded faith: "The Psalms are necessary because they are the prayer masters. . . . We apprentice ourselves to these masters, acquiring facility in using the tools, by which we become more and more ourselves. If we are willfully ignorant of the Psalms, we are not thereby excluded from praying, but we will have to hack our way through formidable country by trial and error and with inferior tools."[2]

Indeed, the Psalter is the foundational and paradigmatic prayer book of the Christian church. Time and time again, worshiping communities have returned to the Psalter for inspiration and instruction in the life of both personal and public prayer. Some of the most auspicious liturgical reform movements in church history — including those of sixth-century monastic communities, sixteenth-century Lutherans and Calvinists, and the twentieth-century Liturgical Movement — have called for a renewed appreciation for the liturgical possibilities of the Psalter.[3] Early African-American expressions of Christian worship were known for "a kind of extatic Delight in Psalmody,"[4] and the Psalms are also both a point of comparison for understanding black spirituals and a source of inspiration for recent black gospel music.[5] If we want to better understand the DNA of the Christian faith and to deepen our worship, there are few better places to begin than with careful and prayerful engagement with the Psalms.

At root, this conviction arises from the place of the Psalms within the canon of Scripture. The Psalms, like all Scripture, are "inspired by God and

2. Eugene Peterson, *Answering God: The Psalms as Tools for Prayer* (San Francisco: Harper and Row, 1989), p. 4.

3. For a fascinating history on the use of the Psalter, see William Holladay, *The Psalms Through Three Thousand Years* (Minneapolis: Fortress Press, 1993).

4. Rev. Samual Davies, letter of 1755, in Eileen Southern, ed., *Readings in Black American Music* (New York: Norton, 1983), pp. 27-28. For further discussion, see Melva Wilson Costen, *In Spirit and In Truth: The Music of African American Worship* (Louisville: Westminster John Knox Press, 2004), pp. 34, 48, 141; Christopher Small, *Music of the Common Tongue: Survival and Celebration in African American Music* (Hanover, NH: Wesleyan University Press, 1987), ch. 3, and several references indexed in Eileen Southern, *The Music of Black Americans: A History,* 3rd ed. (New York: Norton, 1997); William T. Dargan, *Lining Out the Word: Dr. Watts Hymn Singing in the Music of Black Americans* (Berkeley: University of California Press, 2006), pp. 90-100.

5. Glenn Hinson, *Fire in My Bones: Transcendence and the Holy Spirit in African American Gospel* (Philadelphia: University of Pennsylvania Press, 2000), pp. 46-48.

Other Biblical Canticles

The broad themes of this volume can also be easily applied to our study and use of other biblical canticles, including — to name only a few of the more famous examples — the song of Miriam (Exod. 15:1-18); the song of Deborah (Judges 5); the song of Hannah (1 Sam. 2:1-10); the songs of David (2 Sam. 22:2-51, 1 Chron. 16:8-36); various canticles of Isaiah (see Isaiah 12; 25); the book of Lamentations; the song of Mary, the Magnificat *(Luke 1:46-55); the song of Zechariah, the* Benedictus *(Luke 1:68-79); and the song of Simeon, the* Nunc Dimittis *(Luke 2:29-32).*

useful for teaching, for reproof, for correction, and for training in righteousness, so that everyone who belongs to God may be proficient, equipped for every good work" (2 Tim. 3:16-17). The words of the Psalter are reliable and trustworthy, though to be sure, they can also be challenging, perplexing, and even disturbing. For several commentators throughout the history of the church, this conviction suggested that praying the Psalms was one of the best ways to pray "in the Spirit" (Eph. 6:18; Jude 1:20). Indeed, when we pray these texts we are, in a profound if elusive sense, praying the words the Spirit has given us. In the words of Thomas Merton, "Nowhere can we be more certain that we are praying with the Holy Spirit than when we pray the Psalms."[6] In John Calvin's words, when the psalms were sung, "we are certain that God has put the words in our mouths as if they themselves sang in us to exalt his glory."[7]

Yet the Church has not always been a good steward of the Psalms as liturgical prayer. For one, we are often guilty of speaking the strange words of a lament or enthronement Psalm without serious attempts to help worshipers understand what they are saying. Here we might be helped by John Cassian's ancient advice that it might be "better to sing ten verses with a modicum of

6. Thomas Merton, *Praying the Psalms* (Collegeville, MN: Liturgical Press, 1956), p. 18.
7. "La forme des prieres et chantz ecclesiastiques," OS 2:17; trans. Ford Lewis Battles, "John Calvin: The Form of Prayers and Songs of the Church," *Calvin Theological Journal* 15 (1980): 160-65.

comprehension than to pour out the whole psalm with a distracted mind."[8] For another, we often render the Psalms in remarkably unimaginative ways. Over three generations ago, Earle Bennet Cross contended: "It is deplorable to waste the art and beauty of the Psalms on the desert air of systems of responsive readings which bore so many congregations to somnolence."[9] This critique is as relevant today as it was then.

Thoughtful, prayerful use of the Psalms in both public worship and personal devotion requires theological poise, pastoral perception, and artistic imagination — all grounded in the texts themselves. So before we study practical options for reading, singing, and praying the Psalms in worship, it is valuable to pause and consider the way in which the Psalms form us for prayer. The Psalms teach us what faith-filled prayer looks like. They provide what might be called the deep grammar or the paradigmatic structure for Christian prayer.[10]

Consider the following seven lessons the Psalms teach us about prayer. In each case, I briefly describe the lesson and then point to examples of how that lesson is reflected in Christian worship practices. Indeed, the Psalms reflect an ancient, biblical way of praying that continues to shape Christian worship, even when the Psalms themselves are not used. Understanding the nature of that formation will help us both deepen our practice of worship generally and be better stewards of the Psalms themselves.

8. John Cassian, *The Institutes,* trans. Boniface Ramsey, O.P., Ancient Christian Writers, vol. 58 (New York: Newman Press, 2000), II.XI, p. 44.

9. Earle Bennet Cross, *Modern Worship and the Psalter* (New York: Macmillan, 1932).

10. This is roughly similar to the point made by Thomas F. Torrance, that the "basic patterns of worship which we find set out in the ancient liturgy or in the Psalms" are one of the "permanent structures of thought and speech" about God "mediated first to Israel" (*The Mediation of Christ* [Grand Rapids: Eerdmans, 1983], p. 28). Note that this statement could also be made about Jewish worship. An intriguing area for future research would be to compare not only how the Psalms function in Jewish and Christian worship, but also how the Psalms influence the forms, patterns, and theological content of both Jewish and Christian worship. This inquiry might begin with sources such as Stefan C. Reif, *Judaism and Hebrew Prayer: New Perspectives on Jewish Liturgical History* (Cambridge, UK: Cambridge University Press, 1993); Judith H. Newman, *Praying by the Book: The Scripturalization of Prayer in Second Temple Judaism* (Atlanta: Scholars Press, 1999), especially the sources described on pp. 221-41.

1. Personal Address and Dialogic Structure

The biblical Psalms teach us that prayer and worship are not monologues. Rather, in the memorable words of Augustine, Benedict, Cassian, and Calvin, prayer is a "conversation with God."[11] The Psalms themselves are often scripts of conversations. Often they express prayer, words *to* God. At other times, they depict proclamation, words *from* God. Petitions alternate with oracles. Psalm 12, for example, begins with the plea: "Help, O LORD, for there is no longer anyone who is godly." This plea is soon interrupted by an oracle: "'Because the poor are despoiled . . . I will rise up,' says the LORD." This alternation of speakers depicts what Raymond Jacques Tournay has called the "prophetic liturgy of the temple."[12] The Psalms teach us, to use Walter Brueggemann's phrase, that "biblical faith is uncompromisingly and unembarrassedly dialogical."[13] This, in turn, reflects the larger pattern of covenant reciprocity that undergirds large portions of both Old and New Testaments. There is nothing impersonal about biblical faith, and nothing impersonal about biblical worship. Worship is more than mere contemplation of timeless truth; it is a personal encounter between God and the gathered congregation. We can think of it as the exchange of messages between God and the community of faith.

This understanding of worship as interpersonal encounter is a frequently used metaphor for Christian liturgy across traditions. Orthodox, Catholic, and Protestant liturgical theologians have all been known to speak of liturgy as dialogue, as the mutual exchange between God and the community of believers, mediated through the forms of human speech, visual arts, and music. In wor-

11. See John Calvin, *Institutes of the Christian Religion* [1559], ed. John T. McNeill, trans. Ford Lewis Battles, *Library of Christian Classics,* vols. 20-21 (Philadelphia: The Westminster Press, 1960), III.20.4, and the accompanying note. See also Patrick D. Miller, *They Cried to the Lord* (Minneapolis: Fortress Press, 1994), p. 33; Samuel E. Balentine, *Prayer in the Hebrew Bible* (Minneapolis: Fortress Press, 1993), pp. 261-64, Luis Alonso Schökel, *A Manual of Hebrew Poetics* (Rome: Editrice Pontifico Instituto Biblico, 1988), pp. 170-79.

12. Raymond Jacques Tournay, *Seeing and Hearing God with the Psalms: The Prophetic Liturgy of the Second Temple in Jerusalem* (Sheffield: JSOT Press, 1991).

13. Walter Brueggemann, "From Hurt to Joy, From Death to Life," in *The Psalms and the Life of Faith* (Minneapolis: Fortress Press, 1995), p. 68; "Report of the Liturgical Committee," *1968 Acts of Synod of the Christian Reformed Church in North America* (Grand Rapids: CRC Board of Publications, 1968) and in *Psalter Hymnal Supplement* (Grand Rapids: CRC Board of Publications, 1974), pp. 70-75.

ship, we speak to God through prayers, including sung prayers, and in our of-ferings. In worship, God also speaks to us through the reading and preaching of Scripture, including the readings of Scripture that function as calls to wor-ship, words of assurance, and benedictions. God also works to assure and chal-lenge us through songs and artworks, testimonies and greetings. In worship God speaks to us; and we speak to God.

2. IDENTIFYING GOD'S CHARACTER THROUGH METAPHOR AND HISTORICAL RECITATION

Hebrew prayer is addressed to a specific and known God rather than an amor-phous divine being. As Brueggemann points out, "Israel's prayer consists in the utterance of 'you,' addressed to a named, known, addressable, reachable You."[14] This is a particular God, YHWH, whom Christians identify further as the God of Jesus Christ, the one Jesus called "Abba" (e.g., Mark 14:36).

The Psalms specify God's character in at least two ways. First, they draw on a large range of metaphors to speak about God. In the words of William P. Brown, "a storehouse of metaphors both target the deity and tease the reader. In the judicial area, God is judge, advocate, scribe, and bounty hunter, as well as attacker. From a more personally poignant standpoint, God is guide and partner, as well as sun, weaver, and procreator. . . . Yet for the all the iconic characteristics ascribed to the divine, the Psalmist . . . never loses sight of God's unattainable transcendence."[15]

By definition, metaphors "both lie and tell the truth"; by comparison, they illuminate at least one aspect of divine character. But not every aspect of each metaphor is significant or illuminating. For example, calling God "a rock" implies that God is steadfast and faithful, but not lifeless. Naming God as

14. Walter Brueggemann, "The Psalms as Prayer," in *The Psalms and the Life of Faith*, p. 37.

15. William P. Brown, *Seeing the Psalms: A Theology of Metaphor* (Louisville: Westmin-ster John Knox Press, 2002), p. 212. See also Leland Ryken, "Metaphor in the Psalms," in *Christianity and Literature* 31 (1982): 9-30; Barbara P. Green, O.P., *Like a Tree Planted: An Explora-tion of Psalms and Parables Through Metaphor* (Collegeville, MN: Liturgical Press, 1997).

almighty speaks of divine capacity for action, but does not entail that God is ruthless in the exercise of power.[16]

One salient feature of these metaphors is their sheer number and range. The Psalms speak of God as the king, the Lord of hosts, mighty one, but also as shepherd, refuge, "my light," and portion. These metaphors complement and correct each other to depict a God with vast power, but a God who often deploys this power in surprisingly tender ways.

A Sampling of Names for God in the Psalms

This list includes one scriptural reference for each term, though several of these forms of address are used multiple times.

O God of my right (Ps. 4:1)

My King and my God (Ps. 5:2)

O Lord my God (Ps. 7:1)

O righteous God (Ps. 7:9)

Lord, the Most High (Ps. 7:17)

O Lord, our Sovereign (Ps. 8:1)

My rock (Ps. 28:1)

God of Israel (Ps. 41:13)

Lord God of hosts (Ps. 59:5)

God of our salvation (Ps. 65:5)

O Holy One of Israel (Ps. 71:22)

O Shepherd of Israel (Ps. 80:1)

God of vengeance (Ps. 94:1)

Judge of the earth (Ps. 94:2)

Mighty King (Ps. 99:4)

Lover of justice (Ps. 99:4)

---

16. For more on metaphor, see Mark Searle, "Liturgy as Metaphor" in "Language and Metaphor," a theme issue of *Liturgy: Journal of the Liturgical Conference* 4, no. 4 (1985); Gail Ramshaw, *Christ in Sacred Speech* (Philadelphia: Fortress Press, 1986), and *Liturgical Language: Keeping It Metaphoric, Making It Inclusive* (Collegeville, MN: Liturgical Press, 1996); Janet Soskice, *Metaphor and Religious Language* (Oxford: Clarendon Press, 1965), and Witvliet, "Metaphor in Liturgical Studies: Lessons from Philosophical and Theological Theories of Language," *Liturgy Digest* 4, no. 1 (1997): 7-45.

A shield around me (Ps. 3:3)
My glory (Ps. 3:3)
A righteous judge (Ps. 7:10)
King (Ps. 10:16)
Rock (Ps. 18:2)
Fortress (Ps. 18:2)
Deliverer (Ps. 18:2; 144:2)
Horn of my salvation (Ps. 18:2)
Stronghold (Ps. 18:2)
Redeemer (Ps. 19:14)
Shepherd (Ps. 23:1)
God of Jacob (Ps. 24:6)
King of glory (Ps. 24)
God of glory (Ps. 29:3)
Lord of hosts (Ps. 24:10)
God of my salvation (Ps. 25:5)
My light (Ps. 27:1)
My salvation (Ps. 27:1)
My strength/strength of his people (Ps. 28:7-8)
Saving refuge of his anointed (Ps. 28:8)
Help in trouble (Ps. 46:1)
Helper (Ps. 54:4)
Mighty one (Ps. 50:1)
Upholder of my life (Ps. 54:4)
Refuge (Ps. 62:8)
God of Sinai (Ps. 68:8)
Almighty (Ps. 68:14)
Mighty one of Jacob (Ps. 132:2)
Hope (Ps. 71:5)
Trust (Ps. 71:5)
Portion (Ps. 73:26)
Father (Ps. 89:26)
Great God (Ps. 95:3)
Great King above all gods (Ps. 95:3)
Maker (Ps. 95:6)

Lord of all the earth (Ps. 97:5)

Keeper (Ps. 121:5)

Shade at your right hand (Ps. 121:5)

God of gods (Ps. 136:2)

Lord of lords (Ps. 136:3)

God of heaven (Ps. 136:26)

Second, Psalms specify divine character by rehearsing God's deeds in history. Large portions of Hebrew prayer are devoted to recounting the history of God's actions (which God presumably already knows!). This act of remembrance does much more than merely tell a story. It gives identity and specificity to the God who is addressed in prayer, and, correspondingly, to the people who pray.[17] The historical Psalms, such as Psalm 105, are certainly paradigmatic examples of this. Yet this specificity of address and recital of God's deeds can be observed widely in other texts as well.[18] Both Psalms of lament and praise rehearse the acts of God in history. In lament, the Psalmist recites history in order to petition God to be faithful to that same history (see Psalms 85 and 89). In praise and thanksgiving, particularly declarative praise, the Psalmist names the specific acts of God that elicit thankfulness (see Psalms 66, 116, 118, and 138). Especially important is the preposition "for" (Hebrew: *kî*), which signals the listing of specific acts of God (30:2, 116:2, 138:2). God's saving work in the exodus is particularly significant, especially in Psalms 77, 78, 105, 106, and 114. Psalmic praise teaches us to render praise *for* something in particular to a God who has acted in particular, historical ways.

This literary feature corresponds to a central theological theme in many definitions of Christian worship. A chorus of voices gives testimony to this central theme. Roman Catholic systematic theologian Catherine LaCugna argues, for example, that "the trinitarian character of Christian liturgy is to be sought and located in the fact that liturgy, by definition, is the ritual celebration of the events of the economy of redemption and as such is the celebration

17. This is a much-discussed concept among liturgical scholars. See also Brevard Childs, *Memory and Tradition in Israel* (London: SCM Press, 1962); Peter Atkins, *Memory and Liturgy: The Place of Memory in the Composition and Practice of Liturgy* (Aldershot: Ashgate, 2004).

18. Robert Alter, *The Art of Biblical Poetry* (New York: Basic Books, 1985), p. 39.

of the mystery of God."[19] John Burkhart posits that "true worship celebrates the most definite God of the covenant in Moses and Jesus, the God of Abraham, Isaac, and Jacob, of Sarah, Rebekah, and Rachel, and of countless others. Fundamentally, worship is the celebrative response to what God has done, is doing, and promises to do."[20] Nicholas Wolterstorff concurs: "A striking feature of the Christian liturgy is that it is focused not just on God's nature but on God's actions; and more specifically, on actions which took place in historical time."[21] The rehearsal of God's actions in history is commonly accepted as a fundamental component of Christian liturgy.

This point can be cast in boldest relief by contrasting narrative worship with some alternatives. Worship oriented to God's actions in history stands in contrast with ahistorical mystical introspection that seeks an experience of God apart from historical time, and often posits a God beyond the divine economy. Commenting on mysticism in the interpretation of Paul, Lewis Smedes argues that "oriental mysticism could not tolerate dependence on specific historical events or concrete historical personalities. The one thing people need is to escape the concrete things of history and to be immersed into the divine life. . . . Mysticism and history were incompatible as foundations of religion."[22] Donald Bloesch distinguishes ahistorical mysticism from acts of med-

19. Catherine Mowry LaCugna, "Trinity and Liturgy," in *The New Dictionary of Sacramental Worship*, ed. Peter E. Fink (Collegeville, MN: Liturgical Press, 1990), pp. 1293-96; see also "Making the Most of Trinity Sunday," *Worship* 60 (1986): 211.

20. John E. Burkhart, *Worship* (Philadelphia: The Westminster Press, 1982), pp. 17, 31-33.

21. Nicholas Wolterstorff, "The Remembrance of Things (Not) Past: Philosophical Reflections on Christian Liturgy," in *Christian Philosophy*, ed. Thomas P. Flint (Notre Dame, IN: University of Notre Dame Press, 1990), p. 128. Wolterstorff suggests that the absence of commemoration-memorializing in Christian liturgy likely signals the influence of "immediately experiential, or abstractly theological or ethical, approaches to God" (p. 142). He points out that Immanuel Kant believed both that God could not act in history and that traditional liturgy would fade away because it was so bound up with remembrance of God acting in history.

22. Lewis Smedes, *Union with Christ: A Biblical View of New Life in Christ* (Grand Rapids: Eerdmans, 1983), p. 28; and Donald Bloesch, *The Struggle of Prayer* (San Francisco: Harper and Row, 1980), p. 21. Note in this paragraph the significance of the term "ahistorical" to describe one form of mysticism. An element of mystery in worship may be a very good thing, as is a vivid awareness of God's inexhaustibility. The problem comes when a mystical element is set over against an awareness of God's actions in time — past, present, and future.

itation that are "centered on the works and acts of God not only in creation but also and preeminently in Jesus Christ." Any time you hear advice about how prayer "helps us live into the present and escape the past," know that you are leaving the world of Psalmic prayer.

This historical emphasis also stands in contrast to worship practices that merely celebrate nature and nature's annual cycles. Adrio König stresses that ancient Israel changed the calendar of feasts it inherited from its ancient near eastern context from one "linked with nature, into one which was tied to history," and thus transformed what had been celebrations of natural cycles into celebrations of historical events. König argues that this shift in cultic practice corresponded to the theological commitment to conceive of God on the basis of God's action in history.[23] Christians have inherited this historically oriented pattern of liturgy. Christian worship is rooted in history: it is offered to a God who is conceived and named as an agent involved in particular historical events.

In Christian liturgy, the act of remembrance by a recital of God's specific deeds is nowhere more clear than in the emerging eucharistic prayers of the second and third centuries. In Justin Martyr's description of early eucharist, we are told that "the president . . . sends up prayers and thanksgivings to the best of his ability."[24] A key element in the desired charism was the ability to adequately recite the full range of God's deeds in history. Soon, in formalized and prescribed liturgical texts, the prayer of thanksgiving at eucharist consisted largely of an extended recital of God's deeds.

This historical precedent has encouraged modern day liturgists to a renewed appreciation for the structures that accent the narrative recital of God's deeds in history: the Christian year as narrative portrayal of salvation history, baptismal and eucharistic prayers that resemble the narrative prayers of the

23. Adrio König, *Here Am I: A Christian Reflection on God* (Grand Rapids: Eerdmans, 1982), pp. 124, 171.

24. Justin Martyr, *First Apology*, par. 67, *St. Justin Martyr: The First and Second Apologies*, trans. Leslie William Barnard, Ancient Christian Writers, vol. 56 (New York: Paulist Press, 1997), p. 71. See Allan Bouley, O.S.B., *From Freedom to Formula: The Evolution of the Eucharistic Prayer from Oral Improvisation to Written Texts* (Washington, D.C.: The Catholic University of America Press, 1981).

early church, and narrative hymns that recount and extol specific acts of God in creation, redemption, and sanctification.[25]

In each of these ways, Christian liturgy extends a particular pattern of prayer prominent in the Psalter. Whether we lament or praise, we specify the God to whom our prayers are directed by offering biblically grounded names and metaphors for God and naming particular historical deeds our God has enacted. We identify God, we might say, by both nouns and verbs, and thus point to God of both presence and action.

3. The Ebb, Flow, and Fittingness of Praise and Petition, Gratitude and Lament

Psalmic prayer teaches us how to link our praise and petition in fitting ways. Patrick Miller makes the theological point as follows: "Prayer is consistent with the will of God as it seeks something that is consistent with divine nature."[26] Thus, the cry for mercy in Psalm 130 ("Out of the depths I cry to you, O Lord") is dependent on the assertion "but with you there is forgiveness" (v. 4). Psalm 68's urgent plea for God to "summon your power" follows the praise of God for similar actions in the past. Psalm 68:28, in fact, is a key to unlock the logic of vast portions of the Psalter: "Show us your strength, O God, *as you have done before.*" Petition is always grounded in praise. Prayers for God's future work begin with a look into the past.

This has served as a reliable pattern for Christian liturgical prayer as well. Petitions or laments are right and fitting if they can be placed in the context of praise that addresses corresponding characteristics of God. Just as Israel, in Brueggemann's words, "prays God's character back to God, insists that Yahweh be who Yahweh asserted God's own self to be,"[27] so too Christian liturgical

---

25. The recovery of a full anamnesis in the baptismal and eucharistic prayers has been a central feature in recent liturgical reform. See, for example, *The Book of Common Worship* (Louisville: Westminster John Knox Press, 1993), pp. 39, 42-43, 69-70, 410.

26. Patrick D. Miller, *They Cried to the Lord,* p. 321.

27. Brueggemann, "The Psalms as Prayer," p. 47.

prayer looks for ways, in Miller's words, to "ground the petition in the character of God."[28] A clear example of this can be found in the collect prayer form.[29]

A simple collect has four distinct parts to it. First, we *address* God and sometimes *embellish* our calling upon God. For example, a simple address would be simply "O God"; an address with an embellishment might be "O living and loving God." Second, we say something about God: in prayer language this is called an "attribute." For example, at Christmas dinner we might say "O living and loving God, you who sent your only Son to become one like us." Third, we tell God our needs, and ask for God's action, usually expressing a desired result; for example, at Christmas dinner we might say, "Bless this food so that we might be strengthened to bring the light of your Son Jesus to all we meet." Finally, we Christians always pray to the Father through Christ, so we always add this or a similar statement which is called the statement of *mediation:* "We ask this (or grant this) through Christ our Lord," to which we all finally conclude the prayer with "Amen."

The collect form itself, so intimately tied to the poetic qualities of the Latin language, may not be the form of choice for all English-speaking Christians. But it need not be dismissed on the grounds that it is archaic. Indeed, the basic pattern of the collect is even part of colloquial speech. Not long ago, a friend of mine was told, "Ron, you're good at handling technology. Would you scan and e-mail this document to someone, so that we can prepare for our meeting successfully?" Most of the key parts of collect prayer are found in this informal question.[30]

So the lesson of fittingness ought to remain. Like the prayers of the Psalms, the crucial and defining aspect of a given prayer involves both the particular petition that is offered and the way in which God is blessed. The crucial relative clause in the collect that follows the opening address, just like the

---

28. Miller, *They Cried to the Lord,* p. 381, n. 44. Jean-Jacques von Allmen makes the same point as follows: "It is part of the theological meaning of common prayer that it should be controlled by what we know of God's will revealed in Jesus Christ." "The Theological Meaning of Common Prayer," *Studia Liturgica* 10 (1974-76): 129.

29. For a history of this prayer form, see the excellent introduction in A. Corrêa, *The Durham Collectar,* Henry Bradshaw Society, vol. 107 (London, 1991), and *The Collect in Anglican Liturgy: Texts and Sources, 1549-1989* (Collegeville, MN: Liturgical Press, 1994); see also Louis Weil, *Gathered to Pray* (Cambridge, MA: Cowley Publications, 1986), pp. 27-58.

30. Thanks to Clay Schmit and Ron Rienstra for this example.

"In the Psalms, ideas rhyme rather than words."

Bono, in Steve Stockman, *Walk On: The Spiritual Journey of U2*

Psalmic participial phrases that specify God's character, serve to ground petition in praise.

At the same time, none of this should be buttoned down too tightly. The fit between praise and petition does not mean that there is always symmetry between them. Rather, in the Psalms as in daily life, our prayers ebb and flow between praise and lament, gratitude and intercession. Steven Chase speaks of this dynamic in his extended study on prayer:

> Conversation in prayer expands, taking on new meaning and dimension, when we realize, for instance, that adoration implies confession of who we are in relation to God and who God is in relation to the world. In a similar way, praise enters conversation with intercession as we begin to see that what we praise God for can become what we ask for on behalf of others. A petitionary prayer becomes a prayer of thanksgiving as we give thanks in faith, believing that what we ask for will be granted. A thanksgiving prayer becomes a petition as our awareness expands to understand that God's gifts are precisely in line with our needs. As modeled in the Psalms, adoration and praise seem to be intimate partners of lament. And as lament makes its painful arc back to adoration, we begin to see verbal prayer not only as rhythmic but also as a continuum on the circle of conversation.[31]

As we ponder the Psalms, then, as well as our own public worship life, one dynamic to attend to is the movement among these modes of prayer, and the profound ways that each mode of prayer shapes the others.

31. Steven Chase, *The Tree of Life: Models of Christian Prayer* (Grand Rapids: Baker Academic, 2005), p. 95.

4. Individual and Communal Speech

The Psalms teach us the simultaneous distinction and integration of corporate and individual prayer. The balanced life of prayer is not only "I pray" or "we pray"; it is both. The Hebrew Psalter has both personal and communal laments, both personal vows of praise and communal hymns of praise. The two distinct genres of individual and communal prayer remind us that no need is too personal nor is any reason for praise too expansive to be gathered up in prayer.

More profoundly still, the Psalms teach us that even prayers offered in the first person singular are not always soliloquies. "I-Psalms" often express the sentiments not just of an isolated poet, but rather of the entire nation of Israel (e.g., Pss. 3:9; 25:22; 130:8). They are expressions of a corporate personality that is a hallmark of the faith of Israel and a challenge to any culture marked by individualism.

Likewise, Christian prayer is both personal and communal, each with its own characteristics. Liturgical prayer is not individual prayer offered in a public space. It is qualitatively different.[32] Public prayer emphasizes the communal nature — the corporate personality — of the congregation. Like individual prayer, public prayer specifically names the particular pleas of individuals, but accents the corporate dimensions of those concerns.[33] Public prayer challenges individual Christians to think of ways to pray vicariously, on behalf of and in the words of another. Then also, public prayer always views the world through a wide-angle lens. Ideally, the needs and hopes and fears of all sorts of people, and races, and cultures are gathered together in corporate prayer.[34]

Part of this expansive vision comes through the use of the Psalms them-

32. See Paul F. Bradshaw, *Two Ways of Praying* (Nashville: Abingdon Press, 1995), pp. 18, 40-41; Weil, *Gathered to Pray,* pp. 2-20.

33. For example, the individual prayer of a recently divorced Christian and the communal prayers in that person's congregation may both name the same concern; but the former would likely focus on the personal pain of the experience, while the latter might focus on the ways in which the experience wounded the community's experience of shalom.

34. Public prayer ought to be much more than simply an amplified version of the minister's private prayers. See William Willimon, *Preaching and Leading Worship* (Philadelphia: The Westminster Press, 1984), pp. 39-50.

selves. The cadences of this language challenge us when we use them as contemporary prayer, precisely because of their ancient, almost timeless feel. The Psalter is like a cathedral in words. Praying the Psalms challenges us to stretch our internal horizons to sense our solidarity with those who prayed these words over three thousand years ago.

Theologian David Ford has developed this theme in a particularly compelling way:

> [T]he Psalmist's 'I' accommodates a vast congregation of individuals and groups down the centuries around the world today. They are all somehow embraced in this 'I'. A vast array of stories, situations, sufferings, blessings, joys and deaths have been read and prayed into the Psalms by those who have identified with their first person. It amounts to an extraordinarily capacious and hospitable 'I'. . . . It is a feature of good liturgical texts that they allow large numbers of diverse people to identify themselves through them. The liturgical 'I' suggests a conception of selfhood . . . which does not simply see itself as separate from all the other selves and groups worshipping through the same liturgy or the Psalms. Seeing oneself as one among the many who indwell the Psalms by singing them encourages one to consider how the others might be related to oneself. To see (in the flesh or in imagination) the faces of the others who receive and perform their identity through singing the Psalms can lead along the path I have followed through a hospitable self, rejecting idolatries, to a worshipping self for whom the orientation to the face of God and the face of other people is primary.[35]

Ford works this theme into an expansive and joyful vision of divine redemption in musical terms, in which he depicts the redeemed person as the "singing self." Ford's work once more illustrates how the Psalms become part of the DNA of Christian worship, doctrine, and life. Some three thousand years after most of them were written, they are still inspiring significant constructive theological work.

35. David F. Ford, *Self and Salvation: Being Transformed* (New York: Cambridge University Press, 1999), p. 127.

"Of Singing of Psalms. It is the duty of Christians to praise God publickly, by singing of Psalms together in the congregation, and also privately in the family. In singing of Psalms, the voice is to be tuneable and gravely ordered; but the chief care must be, to sing with understanding and with grace in the heart, making melody unto the Lord."

Directory for the Public Worship of God, Westminster Assembly, 1644

5. SPECIFICITY AND GENERALITY IN PRAYER

The Psalms present us with both general, open, and metaphoric speech that can be applied to varied circumstances, as well as event-specific language that may be most pertinent on only one occasion. In Claus Westermann's terms, there is both "declarative" and "descriptive" praise, both event-oriented songs of celebration and expansive paeans of praise. In Psalm 30 we find both — general, descriptive praise ("Sing praises to the LORD," vv. 4-5) and specific declarative praise ("you have drawn me up," vv. 1-3, 6ff.). We also find both in Psalm 83, a communal lament, where the Psalmist prays, generally, "see how your enemies are astir," and specifically, "with one mind they plot together . . . the tents of Edom and the Ishmaelites, of Moab and the Hagrites, Philistia, with the people of Tyre. . . ." Such general language, perfect for repeated use in all circumstances, teaches us the value of familiar and trust-worthy words and phrases that rescue us from endless innovation in liturgical prayer. Specific language teaches us how brutally honest and particular our speech to God can be. As Brueggemann phrases it:

> Israel's prayer — even though stylized and therefore in some ways predictable — is rarely safe, seldom conventional, and never routine. It is characteristically daring, outrageous, and adventuresome. Israel's prayer is indeed limit-language that pushes to the edge of social possibility, of

cultural permit, of religious acceptability, and of imaginative experimentation.[36]

Reliable patterns of general language become the basis for daring liturgical improvisations that respond to specific circumstances. As in jazz music, patterns and improvisation are not competing alternatives; rather, patterns become the necessary foundation for improvisation.

Likewise, well-celebrated Christian worship features a judicious balance of general and specific speech. We use tried and true phrases that imprint themselves on our hearts and burrow into our spiritual bones: "Lift up your heart to the Lord"; "Come, let us worship and bow down"; "Open our lips that our mouths may show forth your praise"; "Our help is the name of the Lord, maker of heaven and earth"; or "We bring a sacrifice of praise." We also use language that is specific. Prayers of intercession name the joys and concerns of particular people and events. Sermons conclude with specific applications for the Christian life.

Our worship suffers when it lacks either kind of language. Without common words and phrases, we are cut off from the biblical and historical roots of our faith. Without specific, event-oriented language, we are left with liturgy removed from our particular time and place.[37]

This penchant for specificity is also what makes liturgical prayer such an indelibly political act. In the Psalms and in Christian liturgy, the fullness of life in the world is not properly left at the door when we enter for worship. No, liturgy must be fully integrated with life in this world. Liturgy and justice are not exclusive concerns.[38] Our praise and thanksgiving rightly names God's goodness to the oppressed (Psalm 146). Our petitions to God specifically call for

---

36. Brueggemann, "The Psalms as Prayer," p. 50.

37. One of the most diagnosable liturgical diseases throughout the history of the church has been the excessive use of cliché-laden, generalized speech. As Claus Westermann has pointed out, the hymns of the Enlightenment period are almost entirely descriptive, while those of Luther are more declarative (*Praise of God* [Richmond, VA: John Knox Press, 1965], pp. 32-33, n. 20). The difference, in part, lies in the immediacy of Luther's prose. It also lies in the eagerness to specify that praise is directed to the God of Abraham, Isaac, Jacob, the Abba of Jesus, our Lord. Christian worship ought to resound with specific reference to the works of God in creation, in the life of Jesus, and in the ongoing presence of the Spirit.

38. Nicholas Wolterstorff, "Justice as a Condition of Authentic Liturgy," *Theology Today* 48 (1991): 6-21.

justice to be promoted and injustice squelched.[39] Brueggemann has suggested that, because of their political ramifications, Psalms such as Psalms 2 and 149 may "be too dangerous to sing in our more bourgeois liturgies."[40] This warning comes as prophetic critique to those of us who lead benign worship services that are content with the status quo or are comfortable leaving our hurts and fears at the sanctuary door.

6. Emotional Engagement and Range

The Psalms convey the whole range of human emotion, from despondent sorrow (Psalm 88) to ecstatic joy (Psalm 47 or 48), from ravaging guilt (Psalm 51) to profound gratitude (Psalm 136). In Calvin's famous phrase, the Psalms are "the anatomy of the soul."[41] They teach us that with the God of the covenant, no human emotion is out of place in prayer.

This emotional range in the Psalms is permission-giving in worship. As Ellen Davis notes, the Psalms "enable us to bring into our conversation with God feelings and thoughts that most of us think we need to get rid of before God will be interested in hearing from us."[42] The Psalms model not only humble gratitude but profound doubt and frustration.

To be sure, the emotional range of the Psalms also can create internal dissonance. The Psalms convey sentiments that not every worshiping community has experienced. Yet even when we are not feeling the profound ecstasy or the deep sorrow of a given Psalm text, the Psalm is forming us. It is allowing us to practice certain moves in our relationship with God. As Davis conveys it, "the

39. See the perceptive comments of C. S. Lewis in *Reflections on the Psalms* (New York: Harcourt Brace Jovanovich, 1958), pp. 9-12. In Lewis's turn of phrase, "Christians cry to God for mercy instead of justice; they [the Psalmists] cried to God for justice instead of injustice" (p. 12).

40. See also his study of Psalms 9 and 10 in *The Psalms and the Life of Faith*, pp. 217-34.

41. Calvin, *Commentary on the Book of Psalms,* vol. 1 (Grand Rapids: Eerdmans, 1948-49), p. xxxvii; see also Howard Neil Wallace, *Words to God, Word from God: The Psalms in the Prayer and Preaching of the Church* (Burlington, VT: Ashgate Publishing, 2005), p. 37.

42. Ellen F. Davis, *Getting Involved with God: Rediscovering the Old Testament* (Cambridge, MA: Cowley Publications, 2001), p. 5.

Psalms instruct our feelings without negating them. They draw upon our particular experience of God as at the same time they expand it exponentially."[43]

For two thousand years, this Psalmic emotional range has challenged and inspired Christian hymn writers, prayer book editors, and worship leaders to develop liturgical language, including language for prayer, that explores the full range of human emotion before God. There are several historical examples of prayers written directly in response to prayers from the Psalms.[44]

Recent years have witnessed a recovery of prayers of lament, generally thought to be a neglected mode of prayer.[45] Popular Christian songwriter Michael Card reflects: "Through [David's] psalms of lament, as perhaps nowhere else in scripture, David reveals a God who uses and utilizes everything, especially pain. All true songs of worship are born in the wilderness of suffering." Card goes on to call for the recovery of lament: "If it is true that we must be conformed to [Jesus'] image, then perhaps we must also learn to speak Jesus' lost language. If we must learn to never let go of God, then the best means, provided by the language of lament, must become ours as well."[46]

---

43. Ellen F. Davis, *Wondrous Depth: Preaching the Old Testament* (Louisville: Westminster John Knox Press, 2005), p. 21. Likewise, Rolf Jacobson suggests that the "cognitive dissonance" we experience when praying the Psalms might be precisely the means through which we grow in the life of prayer ("Burning Our Lamps with Borrowed Oil: The Liturgical Use of the Psalms and the Life of Faith," in Stephen Breck Reid, ed., *Psalms and Practice: Worship, Virtue, and Authority* [Collegeville, MN: Liturgical Press, 2001], pp. 90-98).

44. For example, see I. D. MacFarlane, "Religious Verse in French Neo-Latin Poetry," in *Humanism and Reform: The Church in Europe, England, and Scotland, 1400-1643*, ed. James Kirk (Oxford: Blackwell, 1991); Rikvah Zim, *English Metrical Psalms: Poetry as Praise and Prayer, 1535-1601* (Cambridge, UK: Cambridge University Press, 1987).

45. Of the large and growing bibliography on this theme, see especially Kathleen D. Billman and Daniel L. Migliore, *Rachel's Cry: Prayer of Lament and Rebirth of Hope* (Cleveland: United Church Press, 1999); Sally A. Brown and Patrick D. Miller, eds., *Lament: Reclaiming Practices in Pulpit, Pew, and Public Square* (Louisville: Westminster John Knox Press, 2005); Michael Jinkins, *In the House of the Lord: Inhabiting the Psalms of Lament* (Collegeville, MN: Liturgical Press, 1998); and J. Frank Henderson, *Liturgies of Lament* (Chicago: Liturgy Training Publications, 1994); Carl J. Bosma, "A Close Reading of Psalm 13: Daring to Ask the Hard Questions," in Arie C. Leder, ed., *Reading and Hearing the Word: From Text to Sermon* (Grand Rapids: CRC Publications, 1998), pp. 125-60; see also ch. 2 of Witvliet, *Worship Seeking Understanding* (Grand Rapids: Baker Academic, 2003).

46. Michael Card, *A Sacred Sorrow: Reaching Out to God in the Lost Language of Lament* (Colorado Springs: NavPress, 2005), pp. 63, 138.

As Card (echoing the work of Brueggemann and others) explains, when practiced as an act of faith, lament can be a powerfully healing experience. But even more, the very structure of a lament Psalm forms us in a pattern of God-filled Christian living. Laments, to be sure, begin with a cry against the deplorable human condition, a cry against the painfulness of individual tragedy, a cry against the injustices of society. But laments almost never stay there. Having voiced our pain and struggle, laments then recite God's mighty deeds on our behalf. Remembering these deeds — even in the face of pain and struggle — brings us to praise and thanksgiving for God's fidelity and compassion. Laments give voice to our pain but lead us out of that pain by God's strength. Laments are our great prayers of hope, for they remind us that we belong to God, that God's care will sustain us and protect us, and that God's justice will — in the fullness of time — restore justice. This is the very pattern of our everyday living: from struggle to praise, from pain to remembering God's faithful goodness, from injustice to awe and wonder at the divine majesty.

7. IMAGE AND POETRY IN CHRISTIAN SPEECH

Liturgical prayer is an act of vital imagination. "The church speaks in large, metaphorical phrasings that are evocative, generative, suggestive, and ultimately constitutive but resist every closed meaning," says Brueggemann. "Praise is opposed to memo, even as sacrament opposes technique. Memos reduce, minimize, routinize, and seek to control; this sung poetry leaves things open in respect, awe, and astonishment."[47] Praying the Psalms requires vivid, playful imagination, which makes praying the Psalms liturgically in North America a stubborn counter-cultural act.

The Psalms give us a whole gallery of images or metaphors for use in prayer and preaching. Their expressions rely on evocative use of natural symbols, including chaotic waters, illuminating light, faithful movement of heavenly bodies. Through vivid poetic speech, the Psalms inspire an abandon in the praise of God. They ring with sheer delight in praise of God.[48] They depict a world in which trees clap their hands, in which whales and hippos sing praise, in which all creation is caught up in a symphony of shalom to God. The Psalms, in the words of Gail Ramshaw, are "not only a primer, but something of an encyclopedia of biblical imagery."[49]

On the basis of these precedents, Christian worshipers too have felt freedom to explore a rich variety of ways to express praise to God. Joyful abandon is expressed in exuberant ringing shouts of nineteenth-century African American worshipers and in the final hallelujahs of Handelian choral anthems. Vivid stained glass windows in vast Gothic cathedrals and colorful weavings at remote Mexican pilgrimage sites celebrate the variety and wonder of God's creative power. Congregational offertory dances by Kenyan Catholics and solemn processions in large Presbyterian churches depict in movement the broad sweep of committed faith and worship. After the model of the Psalms themselves, Christian liturgical prayer is called to be vivid, passionate, immediate, and intense, as it embodies the praise and petition of God.

47. Brueggemann, "Praise and the Psalms: A Politics of Glad Abandonment," in *Psalms and the Life of Faith*, p. 125; see also pp. 113, 119-21. On metaphors and images in the Psalms, see, especially, Brown, *Seeing the Psalms;* and Alec Basson, *Divine Metaphors in Selected Hebrew Psalms of Lamentation* (Tübingen: Mohr Siebeck, 2006).

48. For a joyful account discovering delight in the Psalter's praise, see C. S. Lewis, *Reflections on the Psalms*, pp. 45-52, 83, 95-97.

49. Gail Ramshaw, *Treasures Old and New: Images in the Lectionary* (Minneapolis: Fortress Press, 2002); see also Brown, *Seeing the Psalms.*

"I have come to appreciate the power of the 'I' in the Psalms, that flexible little pronoun with its layering of voices. It is the key to the enduring power of the Psalms as models for prayer. When I read or pray a Psalm, the 'I' becomes my own. . . . At the same time, because the Psalms are ancient, because Jews and Christians share these words, these prayers bring to bear a whole community of people, assuring me that I am not the first to feel doubt, terror, anxiety, fury, anger, gratitude, ecstasy. Even the 'I' is a 'we' in other words, thousands of thousands of voices, in many languages, have prayed like this before."

Debra Rienstra, *So Much More: An Invitation to Christian Spirituality*

In at least these seven paradigmatic ways, the patterns of prayer found in the Psalms have shaped and continue to shape Christian praise and lament. Consider then the following seven basic questions to ask of each Psalm:

1. Who is speaking in the Psalm? To whom? Does the speaker change during the course of the Psalm?
2. How does the Psalm identify God? Which metaphors and names does it use? What actions are attributed to divine initiative?
3. What actions does the Psalm convey (praise, thanksgiving, petition, lament)? How are those actions related or linked?
4. Is the Psalm expressing an individual or communal prayer?
5. Does the Psalm use specific or general language?
6. What emotion does the Psalm express?
7. What poetic qualities are particularly compelling and challenging in the text?

And because the Psalms ground so much of the practice of worship, these questions can also be turned into helpful criteria for assessing the practice of worship in any Christian community. Consider asking these questions in a worship committee meeting in your congregation:

1. Does our worship include both our words to God and God's words to us? Do worshipers experience them as such?

2. Do we speak about God with the beauty and range of imagery and actions that the Psalms use?

3. Do we link praise and petition, lament and gratitude in ways that are responsive to our life situation and bear testimony to God's faithfulness?

4. Do we use language in worship that is deeply personal and yet also profoundly communal, linking worshipers within the congregation and with believers in every time and place?

5. Do we use both specific and concrete language in worship and also language that is applicable in every time and place?

6. Do we express the full range of human emotions before God's face?

7. Is our worship poetic and beautiful?

Paying attention to these features suggests how the Psalms can continue to be mentors for liturgical prayer. And when the Psalms themselves do function in worship, we should present them in ways that do not obscure these basic features.

Reformation-Era Testimonies from Luther and Calvin

Martin Luther (1483-1546) Many of the fathers have loved and praised the Book of Psalms above all the other books of the Bible. Although the book itself is a sufficient monument to the writers, we ought to express our own praise and thanks for it. In years gone by, all our attention has been taken up by innumerable legends of saints, many Passionals [accounts of the lives and sufferings of the saints], books of edification, and moral stories, which have been in circulation while this book was put away on the top shelf, and so utterly neglected that scarcely a single psalm was properly understood. Yet the Book of Psalms continued to radiate such a sweet and lovely fragrance that every devout man was sustained and encouraged when he came upon its unfamiliar phrases, and so grew to love it. No books of moral tales and no legends of saints which have been written, or ever will be written, are to my mind as noble as the Book of Psalms; and if my purpose were to choose the best of all the edificatory books, legends of saints, or moral stories, and to have them assembled and presented in the best possible way, my choice would inevitably fall on our present Book.

In it we find, not what this or that saint did, but what the chief of all saints did, and what all saints still do. In it is shown their attitude to God, to their friends, to their foes; and their manner of life and behavior in face of manifold dangers and sufferings. Above all this, the book contains divine and helpful doctrines and commandments of every kind. It should be precious and dear to us if only because it most clearly promises the death and resurrection of Christ, and describes His kingdom, and the nature and standing of all Christian people. It could well be called a "little Bible" since it contains, set out in the briefest and most beautiful form, all that is to be found in the whole Bible, a book of good examples from among the whole of Christendom and from among the saints, in order that those who could not read the whole Bible through would have almost the whole of it in summary form, comprised in a single booklet.

The virtue of the Book of Psalms is unique, and is more finely exhibited than elsewhere when we compare it with the multitude of other books which continually babble about the saints and their doings, but seldom or never quote their words. Here the Book of Psalms is unique. It tastes good and sweet to those who read it, and it gives a faithful record of what the saints did and said: how they communed with God and prayed to Him in the old days, and how such men still commune with Him and pray to Him. In comparison with the Book of Psalms, the other books, those containing the legends of saints and other exemplary matter, depict holy men all with their tongues tied; whereas the Book of Psalms presents us with saints alive and in the round. It is like putting a dumb man side by side with one who can speak: the first is only half alive. Speech is the most powerful and exalted of human faculties. Man is distinguished from animals by the faculty of speech, much more than by shape or form or any other activity. A block of timber can be given a human shape by the art of the woodcarver; and an animal is a man's equal in seeing, hearing, smelling, singing, running, standing, eating, drinking, fasting, thirsting; or in bearing hunger, cold, and hardship.

The Book of Psalms has other excellencies: it preserves, not the trivial and ordinary things said by the saints, but their deepest and noblest utterances, those which they used when speaking in full earnest and all urgency to God. It not only tells what they say about their work and conduct, but also lays bare their hearts and the deepest treasures hidden in their souls: and this is done in a way which allows us to contemplate the causes and the sources of their words and works. In other words, it enables us to see into their hearts and understand the nature of their thoughts; how at heart they took their stand in varying circumstances of life, in danger, and in distress. Legends and moral tales cannot, and do not, do this, and so they make much of the miracles and works of the saints. But it is impossible for me to tell the state of a man's heart by only looking at or hearing about his many remarkable activities. And, just as I would rather hear a saint speak than see his actions, so I would rather look into his heart and the treasures of his soul than listen to his works. What the Book of Psalms gives us in richest measure in regard to the saints is the fullness of certainty as to what they felt in their hearts, and what was the sound of the words which they used in addressing God and their fellow-men.

The human heart is like a ship on a stormy sea driven about by winds blowing from all four corners of heaven. In one man, there is fear and anxiety about impending disaster; another groans and moans at all the surrounding evil. One man mingles hope and presumption out of the good fortune to which he is looking forward; and another is puffed up with a confidence and pleasure in his present possessions. Such storms, however, teach us to speak sincerely and frankly, and make a clean breast. For a man who is in the grip of fear or distress speaks of disaster in a quite different way from one who is filled with happiness; and a man who is filled with joy speaks and sings about happiness quite differently from one who is in the grip of fear. They say that when a sorrowing man laughs or a happy man weeps, his laughter and his weeping do not come from the heart. In other words, these men do not lay bare, or speak of things which lie in, the bottom of their hearts.

The Book of Psalms is full of heartfelt utterances made during storms of this kind. Where can one find nobler words to express joy than in the Psalms of praise or gratitude? In them you can see into the hearts of all the saints as if you were looking at a lovely pleasure-garden, or were gazing into heaven. How fair and charming and delightful are the flowers you will find there which grow out of all kinds of beautiful thoughts of God and His grace. Or where can one find more profound, more penitent, more sorrowful words in which to express grief than in the Psalms of lamentation? In these, you see into the hearts of all the saints as if you were looking at death or gazing into hell, so dark and obscure is the scene rendered by the changing shadows of the wrath of God. So, too, when the Psalms speak of fear or hope, they depict fear and hope more vividly than any painter could do, and with more eloquence than that possessed by Cicero or the greatest of orators. And, as I have said, the best of all is that these words are used by the saints in addressing God; that they speak with God in a tone that doubles the force and earnestness of the words themselves. For when a man speaks to another man on subjects such as these, he does not speak from his deepest heart; his words neither burn nor throb nor press so urgently as they do here.

It is therefore easy to understand why the Book of Psalms is the favourite book of all the saints. For every man on every occasion can find in it Psalms which fit his needs, which he feels to be as appropriate as if they had been set there just for his sake. In no other book can he find words to equal them, nor better words. Nor does he wish it. And there follows from this a further excellence that when some such a word has come home and is felt to answer his need, he receives assurance that he is in the company of the saints, and that all that has happened to the saints is happening to him, because all of them join in singing a little song with him, since he can use their words to talk with God as they did. All this is reserved to faith, for an ungodly man has no idea what the words mean.

Finally, the Book of Psalms contains an assurance and a valid passport with which we can follow all the saints without danger. The moral stories and legends of the saints whose words are never given, advocate works that no man can imitate, works that are, in most cases, the beginnings of sects and factions, that lead and even drag one away from the fellowship of the saints. The Book of Psalms, on the other hand, preserves you from factions and leads you into the fellowship of the saints; for, whether in joy, fear, hope, or sorrow, it teaches you to be equable in mind and calm in word, as were all the saints. The sum of all is that, if you wish to see the holy Christian church depicted in living colours, and given a living form, in a painting in miniature, then place the Book of Psalms in front of you; you will have a beautiful, bright, polished mirror which will show you what Christianity is. Nay, you will see your own self in it, for here is the true γνώθι σεαυτον ["know thyself"], by which you can know yourself as well as the God Himself who created all things.

Let us therefore take care to thank God for these immeasurable benefits. Let us accept, use, and exercise them diligently and earnestly to the glory and honour of God, lest by our ingratitude we earn something worse. For of old, in the dark times, what a treasure it would have been held to be, if a man could have rightly understood one single Psalm, and could have read or heard it in simple German. To-day, however, blessed are the eyes that see what we see and the ears that hear what we hear. But beware (for unfortunately we witness it) lest it happen to us as to the Jews in the wilderness, who said of the heavenly manna, Our soul turns from this poor food. For we ought to understand what is also said, "that they suffered from plagues and died," lest it happen to us, too. To this end, may we be helped by the Father of all grace and mercy through Jesus Christ our Lord, to whom be praise and thanks, honor and glory, for the Book of Psalms in the common German tongue, and for all his innumerable and unutterable mercies for ever. Amen.

Martin Luther, 1528 Preface to the Psalms, in *Martin Luther: Selections from His Writings,* ed. John Dillenberger (New York: Anchor Books, 1961), pp. 37-41

John Calvin (1509-1564) The varied and resplendent riches which are contained in this treasury [of the Psalms] it is no easy matter to express in words; so much so, that I well know that whatever I shall be able to say will be far from approaching the excellence of the subject. But as it is better to give to my readers some taste, however small, of the wonderful advantages they will derive from the study of this book, than to be entirely silent on the point, I may be permitted briefly to advert to a matter, the greatness of which does not admit of being fully unfolded. I have been accustomed to call this book, I think not inappropriately, "An Anatomy of all the Parts of the Soul;" for there is not an emotion of which any one can be conscious that is not here represented as in a mirror. Or rather, the Holy Spirit has here drawn to the life all the

griefs, sorrows, fears, doubts, hopes, cares, perplexities, in short, all the distracting emotions with which the minds of men are wont to be agitated. The other parts of Scripture contain the commandments which God enjoined his servants to announce to us. But here the prophets themselves, seeing they are exhibited to us as speaking to God, and laying open all their inmost thoughts and affections, call, or rather draw, each of us to the examination of himself in particular, in order that none of the many infirmities to which we are subject, and of the many vices with which we abound, may remain concealed. It is certainly a rare and singular advantage, when all lurking places are discovered, and the heart is brought into the light, purged from that most baneful infection, hypocrisy. In short, as calling upon God is one of the principal means of securing our safety, and as a better and more unerring rule for guiding us in this exercise cannot be found elsewhere than in The Psalms, it follows, that in proportion to the proficiency which a man shall have attained in understanding them, will be his knowledge of the most important part of celestial doctrine.

Genuine and earnest prayer proceeds first from a sense of our need, and next, from faith in the promises of God. It is by perusing these inspired compositions, that men will be most effectually awakened to a sense of their maladies, and, at the same time, instructed in seeking remedies for their cure. In a word, whatever may serve to encourage us when we are about to pray to God, is taught us in this book. And not only are the promises of God presented to us in it, but oftentimes there is exhibited to us one standing, as it were, amidst the invitations of God on the one hand, and the impediments of the flesh on the other, girding and preparing himself for prayer: thus teaching us, if at any time we are agitated with a variety of doubts, to resist and fight against them, until the soul, freed and disentangled from all these impediments, rise up to God; and not only so, but even when in the midst of doubts, fears, and apprehensions, let us put forth our efforts in prayer, until we experience some consolation which may calm and bring contentment to our minds. Although distrust may shut the gate against our prayers, yet we must not allow ourselves to give way, whenever our hearts waver or are agitated with inquietude, but must persevere until faith finally come forth victorious from these conflicts. In many places we may perceive the exercise of the servants of God in prayer so fluctuating, that they are almost overwhelmed by the alternate hope of success and apprehension of failure, and gain the prize only by strenuous exertions. We see on the one hand, the flesh manifesting its infirmity; and on the other, faith putting forth its power; and if it is not so valiant and courageous as might be desired, it is at least prepared to fight until by degrees it acquire perfect strength. But as those things which serve to teach us the true method of praying aright will be found scattered through the whole of this Commentary, I will not now stop to treat of topics which it will be necessary afterwards to repeat, nor detain my readers from proceeding to the work itself. Only it appeared to me to be requisite to show in passing, that this book makes known to us this privilege, which is desirable above all others — that not only is there opened up to us familiar access to God, but also that we have permission and freedom granted us to lay open before him our infirmities, which we would be ashamed to confess before men. Besides, there is also here prescribed to us an infallible rule for directing us with respect to the right manner of offering to God the sacrifice of praise, which he declares to be most precious in his sight, and of the sweetest odour. There is no other book in which there is to be found more express and magnificent commendations, both of the unparalleled liberality of God towards his Church, and of all his works; there is no other book in which there is recorded so many deliverances, nor one in which the evidences and experiences of the fatherly providence and solicitude which God exercises towards us, are celebrated with such splendour of diction, and yet with the strictest adherence to truth; in short, there is no other book in which we are more perfectly taught the right manner of praising God, or in which we are more powerfully stirred up to the performance of this religious exercise.

Moreover, although The Psalms are replete with all the precepts which serve to frame our life to every part of holiness, piety, and righteousness, yet they will principally teach and train us to bear the cross; and the bearing of the cross is a genuine proof of our obedience, since by doing this, we renounce the guidance of our own affections, and submit ourselves entirely to God, leaving him to govern us, and to dispose of our life according to his will, so that the afflictions which are the bitterest and most severe to our nature, become sweet to us, because they proceed from him. In one word, not only will we here find general commendations of the goodness of God, which may teach men to repose themselves in him alone, and to seek all their happiness solely in him; and which are intended to teach true believers with their whole hearts confidently to look to him for help in all their necessities; but we will also find that the free remission of sins, which alone reconciles God towards us, and procures for us settled peace with him, is so set forth and magnified, as that here there is nothing wanting which relates to the knowledge of eternal salvation.

John Calvin, *Calvin's Commentaries*, vol. 1 (Grand Rapids: Eerdmans, 1949), pp. xxxvi-xxxix

On the other hand there are the psalms which we desire to be sung in the Church, as we have it exemplified in the ancient Church and in the evidence of Paul himself, who says it is good to sing in the congregation with mouth and heart. We are unable to compute the profit and edification which will arise from this, except after having experimented. Certainly as things are, the prayers of the faithful are so cold, that we ought to be ashamed and dismayed. The psalms can incite us to lift up our hearts to God and move us to an ardour in invoking and exalting with praises the glory of his Name.

John Calvin, "Articles Concerning the Organization of the Church and of Worship at Geneva Proposed by the Ministers at the Council, January 16, 1537," X, I, 5, in *Calvin: Theological Treatises*, ed. J. K. S. Reid (Philadelphia: Westminster Press, 1977), p. 54

PART II

Praying the Psalms in Christian Worship

At their best, the biblical Psalms are meant not only to be studied and preached, but to be read, sung, and prayed. They not only teach us about God, they help us enact our relationship with God. As Ellen Davis phrases it, the Psalms are "packaged ready to be put directly into our mouths. . . . Using their words brings us into direct encounter: through them we find ourselves talking to the living God, sometimes in language we would never have imagined would come from our lips into God's ear."[1]

Preachers and worship leaders need not choose between using the Psalms for preaching or for prayer and praise. Ideally, they should be regularly sung in worship, and at least periodically preached. Even when the Psalms are not preached, there are rich practices of praying the Psalms that complement sermons on other Biblical texts and themes. When they are preached, the sustained attention given to the text opens up several possibilities for both presenting and praying a Psalm in creative ways that can break open the significance of the text for worshipers.

Fortunately, the use of the Psalms in worship does not have to be complicated. In some congregations, the matter is as simple as looking to the lectionary to determine which Psalm to sing in a given week and looking to a hymnal or readily available collection of responsorial Psalms to find a musical

1. Ellen F. Davis, *Getting Involved with God* (Cambridge, MA: Cowley Publications, 2001), p. 9.

setting of that Psalm. In others, it is as simple as looking in one of the many resources described later in this volume to identify a musical style and particular Psalm text that matches the pastoral needs of a congregation on a given week. May the number of congregations who follow these simple procedures increase! Regular reading, singing, and praying from the Psalms is one of the simplest and most effective ways to keep worship grounded in Scripture and to help connect worship with the vast range of personal experience that worshipers bring with them. If we want "authentic" worship, we don't need to search further.

For congregations that already practice regular lectionary-based use of the Psalms in a set liturgy, the following analysis is designed to help make explicit what is already happening implicitly. These congregations have the benefit of working with established patterns that harvest generations of wisdom about which Psalms to use at what time and in what way. The danger these congregations face is that this wisdom is not always accessible. Sometimes historic practices persist, but without any sense of what makes them significant. My hope is that reflection on these themes helps uncover a part of this wisdom. Look in the paragraphs that follow for insights that may help you look at your cherished practices in new ways, or assist you in exploring other methods of speaking, singing, or depicting the Psalms. Indeed, there are many creative and well-grounded possibilities for use of the Psalms in worship that the lectionary and other set patterns of worship leave unexplored.

For the congregations that read, sing, or pray the Psalms only sporadically in worship, or who do not follow a set liturgy or use the lectionary, the following analysis is designed to suggest ways of becoming more intentional about using this remarkable biblical book in worship. These congregations have the freedom to draw on the Psalms in interesting, creative, and pastorally responsive ways that prayer-book congregations may not. The challenge here is that this creativity and responsiveness requires uncommon insight and energy, and careful coordination between the preacher and those who will lead music or other aspects of worship.

The following resources and perspectives focus on using either extended portions of Psalms or entire Psalms, rather than merely a single verse or short portion of a selected Psalm. The evolution of the medieval mass witnessed the attrition of the Psalter from the use of entire Psalms to the use of mere versicles, often sung during the processions at introit and communion.[2] The same process of attrition has occurred in some expressions of recent Protestant congregational song, in which preference is given to singing one scriptural verse several times rather than extended portions of the text. Single verses from the Psalms certainly have their place in worship. They are significant as the texts for simple songs of praise (whether in Scripture choruses or Handelian arias) and for liturgical leaders looking for a good spoken transition. But for too long many traditions have been content to limit the use of Psalm material to a favorite or convenient versicle for liturgical use, totally ignoring the structures and contexts by which these verses gain meaning. (My hope, then, is not to displace the use of single verses or images from the Psalms, but to add to them the reading or singing of longer literary units.)

The bulk of recent scholarly analysis of the Psalms has focused on identifying basic literary structures or patterns in the Psalms and discerning how individual texts improvise within a given structure. One consistent theme throughout this work is that most Psalms convey much of their meaning through movement, by taking us somewhere. They offer more than simply beautiful epigrams or metaphors. As William P. Brown summarizes, the meaning and metaphors of the Psalms forge a theological vision that is "wrought in movement . . . by fits and starts, the pray-er of Psalms is taken from trench to temple, from lament to praise, from 'pathway' to 'refuge.'"[3] This insight suggests the significant value of using larger, rather than smaller portions of Scripture.

Readers may well be surprised by the stylistic breadth of the resources included in this section. They include musical suggestions in classical, jazz, folk, and popular styles, in multiple languages, and textual suggestions in both authorized translations and free paraphrases. I work in an environment with regular contact with congregations across the spectrum of styles and approaches — and see the significant contribution that the Psalms can make to nearly every worshiping community. Whatever our congregational type, we all have much to learn from the Psalms. Indeed, even though they may be three millen-

2. Josef A. Jungmann, *Mass of the Roman Rite: Its Origins and Development* (New York: Benziger Brothers, 1995), p. 34, n. 5.

3. William P. Brown, *Seeing the Psalms: A Theology of Metaphor* (Louisville: Westminster John Knox Press, 2002), p. 215.

nia old, the Psalms are still out ahead of us. We are still growing into them. They are cutting edge material for effective contextual ministry.

The following suggestions briefly consider each step in the process of preparing to pray or sing the Psalms in worship:

- choosing Psalms;
- choosing a Psalm's liturgical placement or function;
- studying the text of the Psalm;
- choosing how to render the Psalms in speech, song, or visual depiction.

Note carefully that the extensive analysis that follows is not meant to suggest that Psalmody needs to be inordinately complicated. I realize that such a detailed process of selecting and preparing Psalms cannot be followed every week in the vast majority of congregations. Still, pausing to reflect on the assumptions built into each step of the process can enhance and discipline the pastoral work of worship leadership over time. Consider giving extended attention to one aspect of the process each week as a way of developing new capacities for effective leadership.

One final note: This material is written out of my great personal enthusiasm for a renewed appreciation for and use of the biblical Psalms. That enthusiasm comes from my experiencing the robust and gritty significance of the Psalms in both worship and personal study and from a vivid awareness of how little the Psalms, especially in longer literary units, are used in worship today in many traditions. I also am aware of some of the possible unintended consequences of this enthusiasm. It is easy to overestimate the significance of the Psalms in earlier periods of church history or to give the impression that their pervasive use is absolutely necessary for vital and faithful worship.[4]

THE INFORMATION LISTED HERE is drawn from a wide range of resources, some of which work with a slightly different numbering of the Psalms. Most common translations reflect the Hebrew numbering of the Psalms (as does this book).

---

4. Thus I am grateful for Paul Bradshaw's work in de-romanticizing our view of psalmody in the early church. See his *Two Ways of Praying* (Nashville: Abingdon Press, 1995), pp. 73-87.

Some translations, however, use a numbering system from the ancient Latin Vulgate translation, which in turn was translated from the Greek version of the Old Testament (the Septuagint), assigning some Psalms a number that is one lower than the Hebrew numbers (Psalms 9–145, except 115–116). So Psalm 42, for example, is Psalm 41 in some sources. This alternate numbering system is found especially in some resources used in Roman Catholic contexts.

1. Choosing a Psalm

Choosing an appropriate Psalm for worship is a challenging and significant task.[5] When we choose a Psalm (or any other prayer or song), we are placing words on the lips of the congregation that shapes their experience of relating to God. This means that our choice of text always needs to take into account not only the text, but also our theology and our awareness of the experience that people bring with them to worship. Consider three broad types of rationale that inform the choice of a Psalm: liturgical, homiletical, and pastoral.

Liturgical Criteria

In many contexts, the obvious way to choose a Psalm is simply to find one that says what we want to say. If we want to praise, we sing Psalm 98. If we want to repent, we pray Psalm 51. If we want to lament, we use Psalm 13. So when we have firmly in mind what we want a Psalm to accomplish in worship, we set off on a search. We thumb through our Bibles until we come upon a text that more or less fits our purposes. Task accomplished.

While this may be effective for planning a particular service, the results of using this method exclusively over time are not altogether promising. Often

5. For historical perspectives on this, see J. A. Lamb, *The Psalms in Christian Worship* (London: Faith Press, 1962); Massey H. Shepherd Jr., *The Psalms in Christian Worship: A Practical Guide* (Minneapolis: Augsburg, 1976); and Aimé-Georges Martimort, "Fonction de la Psalmodie dans la liturgie de la Parole," in *Mirabile Laudis Canticum* (Rome: Edizioni Liturgiche, 1991), pp. 75-96.

this method results in a severely restricted use of the Psalms. Certain favorite Psalms are used a great deal to the virtual exclusion of others.

Another danger of this ad hoc approach is the tendency to choose texts that are only generally applicable. Worship leaders in a wide spectrum of congregations tend to choose the Psalm texts that feature the most general language, such as "Sing to the Lord a new song," "The Lord is my shepherd," or "Create in me a clean heart." These are certainly significant, paradigmatic Psalm texts, worthy of repeated and sustained use. But if those are the only kinds of texts chosen, after a while all the Psalms sound alike. If we don't choose a text for a very specific reason (and communicate that reason), then these prized poetic expressions, with their profound parallelisms and vivid images, can become a sea of clichés in our worship. If, after years and years of eager and well-intentioned participation in public worship, veteran Christians have only a vague memory of using small parts of Psalm 103 and maybe, on a deep day, Psalm 51, then something is seriously wrong with their congregation's liturgical diet.

Further, this approach can, without care, perpetuate the impression that worship — and the liturgical use of biblical materials — relies on language that only expresses the praise, petition, and lament we already previously have felt, forgetting that worship also needs to teach us to say things that don't come naturally to us. Worship, that is, should not only express our prayer, but form us to pray more deeply.[6] If this is to happen, we must learn to pray the Psalms that we otherwise might not so readily choose.

And even if we never end up using a particular Psalm to express "authentically" our own internal emotional states, it is of benefit for us to pray them in solidarity with others in the body of Christ. At any given moment, no one person or group of persons is feeling and experiencing all the emotions that are represented in the Psalter, but at any given moment, some people are experiencing this or that facet of the Psalms (and eventually we all will have these experiences somewhere along the way). The Psalms are varied so as to give voice to life's many seasons.[7]

6. Such is the advice of countless wise veterans of Christian prayer, such as Bonhoeffer: "We also ought not to select Psalms at our own discretion, thinking that we know better what we ought to pray than does God himself." *Psalms: Prayerbook of the Bible* (Minneapolis: Augsburg, 1970), p. 26.

7. I am grateful to Scott Hoezee for helping me express this point.

All of this suggests the value of some regular regimen of praying the Psalter, some way of ensuring that we will use a larger portion of the Psalms. Indeed, there is precedent for a regular pattern of Psalm selection in most worship traditions. In the Middle Ages, Benedictine monks prayed the Psalms each week in a particular order. In Calvin's Geneva, despite the rejection of the Roman lectionary for Scripture readings and sermon texts, the Psalms were sung in public worship according to a regular regimen that was printed in the back of the published Psalters (indeed, it was a lectionary for singing).[8] Long before the day of thematic worship planning, Reformed worshipers sang whatever Psalm came next in the regular order, rather than Psalms chosen to correspond with the sermon or because they were a favorite of members of the congregation. In twentieth-century liturgical renewal, the Psalms have again been featured as a vital part of the lectionary, which disciplines the use of Scripture in many worshiping communities. This discipline results in exposure to a far greater number and range of Psalms than usually results when Psalms are chosen for occasional use at the discretion of a given pastor or worship leader. Such discipline has much to commend it.

There are several possible regimens for choosing Psalms.

CANONICAL ORDER

One obvious method would simply be to pray the Psalms, both privately and communally, in canonical order. This is the least common regimen evidenced in the history of worship (though it has been practiced in some monastic communities). Yet, given the remarkable scholarly energy in the past generation that has uncovered the genius of the organization and editing of the Psalter as a complete book, the practice of reading or praying the Psalms in canonical order would be an appropriate spiritual discipline for individuals or a congregation. Just as reading Romans from beginning to end helps us sense the logic of its overall structure (from sin to grace to service) and offers a framework for interpreting specific texts, so praying the Psalter from beginning to end helps us sense its ebbs and flows. Doing this would help us feel the crescendo of the Psalter as it moves from a relatively high percentage of lament Psalms (Books

---

8. Pierre Pidoux, *Le Psautier huguenot du XVIe siècle* (Basel, 1962), vol. 2, pp. 45, 63, 135.

I-III) to nearly exclusively Psalms of praise (Book V), and from a relatively high percentage of individual expressions to many more communal exclamations.[9] A Psalm-by-Psalm canonical reading also helps us sense the powerful (perhaps quite intentional) juxtaposition of particular Psalms. Here is a small sampling of observations about the shaping of the Psalter:

- Psalms 1 and 2 are a theologically significant introduction to the entire Psalter.
- The wonder expressed in Psalm 8 is more pronounced because it is framed by five lament Psalms.
- Psalms 42 and 43 are linked by a common refrain.
- The despair of Psalm 88 is followed by the covenant hope of Psalm 89.
- Psalms 145–150 function as a doxological conclusion to the entire collection.

As with any other part of Scripture, the meaning of individual Psalms is communicated in part through its literary context.

THE LECTIONARY AND THE CHRISTIAN YEAR

Each of the major lectionaries published in the last forty years, including the Revised Common Lectionary, includes a selection from the Psalms as one of the assigned texts for each week. For the Revised Common Lectionary, the Psalms are chosen primarily to function as a response to the designated reading from the Old Testament, rather than to serve primarily as the best psalmic counterpart to the New Testament Gospel readings (though often there is natural correspondence between the Psalm and the New Testament or Gospel reading).[10]

9. See Gerald H. Wilson, *The Editing of the Hebrew Psalter* (Macon, GA: Mercer University Press, 1997); see also Wilson, "The Shape of the Book of Psalms," *Interpretation* 46 (1992): 138-39; Nancy L. deClaissé-Walford, *Reading from the Beginning: The Shaping of the Hebrew Psalter* (Macon, GA: Mercer University Press, 1997), and *Introduction to the Psalms: A Song from Ancient Israel* (St. Louis: Chalice Press, 2004); and J. Clinton McCann, ed., *The Shape and Shaping of the Psalter* (Sheffield, UK: Sheffield Academic Press, 1993).

10. Horace T. Allen Jr., "The Psalter in the Revised Common Lectionary (1992)," *Reformed Liturgy and Music* 26 (1992): 84-85. See the *General Instruction of the Roman Missal* (Washington, DC: United States Catholic Conference, 2000), para. 61. For more background on the logic of the lectionary, see Fritz West, *Scripture and Memory: The Ecumenical Herme-*

Several lectionary choices also reflect historically significant Psalms for a given day in the Christian year (Psalm 22, for example, has been a Psalm of choice for Good Friday all the way back to the extant lectionaries from the early church).

For congregations that do follow the lectionary, the Psalms can be approached as much more than a response to the Old Testament reading. As Paul Westermeyer suggests, "The singing of a Psalm between the OT and Epistle functions to call to mind the whole story, the whole *Heilsgeschichte*, the whole panorama of salvation history. The Psalms allow us to sing the church's ballad, structured with a telos of Gospel. The lessons and the sermon are laser-like shafts of light that illumine the whole Psalmic story and our places in it; but the paradoxical reverse is also true: the Psalmic story itself provides context and makes it possible for the laser-like shafts to shine at all."[11] The Psalms also often introduce the language of personal or communal prayer into the set of Scripture selections for the day. The juxtaposition of psalmic poems with Old Testament and Gospel narrative and epistolary exposition creates a fertile mix of rhetoric to shape the congregation's prayer.

Congregations who follow the lectionary should be aware that even scrupulous attention to most lectionaries' Scripture selections will allow them to pray only a portion of the Psalms. The longer Psalms especially are truncated to fit what is perceived to be a manageable portion for a given service. This limitation is, of course, avoidable. Congregations that do not follow the lectionary usually use even less of the Psalter than those who do. This should, however, suggest why it is important for lectionary users to look for ways of praying and singing Psalms not only in conjunction with the Scripture readings, but also as opening hymns of praise, communion or baptismal songs, and even as part of congregational prayers of intercession, confession, or thanksgiving.

---

neutic of the Three-Year Lectionaries (Collegeville, MN: Liturgical Press, 1997); Norman Bonneau, *The Sunday Lectionary: Ritual Word, Paschal Shape* (Collegeville, MN: Liturgical Press, 1998); and especially Irene Nowell, *Sing a New Song: The Psalms in the Sunday Lectionary* (Collegeville, MN: Liturgical Press, 1993).

11. Paul Westermeyer, personal correspondence, June 1, 2006. For more on the logic of lectionary choices, see Irene Nowell, *Sing a New Song: The Psalms in the Sunday Lectionary* (Collegeville, MN: Liturgical Press, 1993), and Margaret Daly-Denton, "Psalmody as the 'Word of Christ,'" in *Finding Voice to Give God Praise: Essays in the Many Languages of the Liturgy* (Collegeville, MN: Liturgical Press, 1998), 73-86.

For congregations that do not follow it, the lectionary is still a source of significant wisdom. First, whenever the sermon is based on an Old Testament text included somewhere in the lectionary, then the lectionary will usually suggest a Psalm that is especially appropriate as a response to the text. Any preacher preparing a sermon on an Old Testament text is wise to consult the lectionary to see what Psalm it suggests.

The Revised Common Lectionary is a good source for locating which Psalms have been traditionally associated with particular events in the life of Christ or season of the year.[12] It reminds us of the appropriateness of, for example, these choices:

Advent[13]	Psalm 24 ("Lift up your heads . . . that the King of glory may come in") and Psalm 80 ("Awaken your might, come and save us")
Christmas	Psalms 96, 97, 98 ("the LORD has made his salvation known") [note: Isaac Watts's famous carol, "Joy to the World," is based on Psalm 98]
Epiphany	Psalm 72 ("All nations will be blessed by him")
Ash Wednesday and Lent	Psalm 51 ("Create in me a clean heart, O God")
Palm Sunday	Psalm 118 ("Hosanna in the highest")
Maundy Thursday	One or more of the Hallel Psalms (Psalms 113–118), the Psalms that may have been sung in the traditional Passover celebration
Good Friday	Psalm 22 ("My God, my God, why have you forsaken me?")
Easter	Psalm 118 ("The stone the builders rejected has become the capstone") and Psalm 16 ("You will not let your Holy One see decay")

12. See *The Worship Sourcebook* (Grand Rapids: Faith Alive/Baker Books, 2004) for extensive Psalms materials for each element of worship and each season of the church year.

13. See Garth Gillan, "Psalmody and the Celebration of Advent," *Worship* 80 (2006): 402-12.

Ascension Day	Psalm 47 ("God has gone up with a shout")
Pentecost	Psalm 104 (with its prayer for the Spirit to "renew the face of the earth")

Suppose a congregation not using the lectionary chose to feature a given biblical Psalm during a season of the year, reading or singing that Psalm weekly over a period of weeks (this may also be a wise idea for congregations that do follow the lectionary). In that case, the lectionary would be one of the best places to consult to identify seasonally appropriate Psalmody. It would, for example, suggest seasonally appropriate Psalms for Advent (Psalms 25, 72, or 80), Lent (Psalms 32, 51, 126, or 130), and Eastertide (16, 23, 30, 47, or 93).

LITURGICAL ELEMENTS AND TYPES OF SERVICES

One unintended effect of lectionary use in some traditions and congregations is to limit the use of the Psalms to one moment in worship (typically between the Old and New Testament readings). Yet there are beautiful and appropriate Psalm texts for nearly every element in worship:

Calls to Worship	Psalms 47, 66, 95, 96, 98, 100, 113, 150 (and many more). The Roman Catholic Sacramentary, for example, has introit Psalm verses assigned for every Mass.
Prayers of Confession	Psalms 6, 32, 38, 51, 102, 130, 143 (the seven penitential Psalms)
Prayers of Lament	Psalms 6, 13, 22, 42 (and many more)
Words of Assurance	Psalms 30, 32, 103
Lord's Supper	Psalms 34, 103, 116.[14] Note also that the Roman Catholic

14. Ideally, these Psalms become closely associated with particular liturgical acts: Dutch Calvinists have traditionally used Psalm 103 after the Lord's Supper, while some Scottish Presbyterians used Psalm 24 before it. See A. C. Honders, "Remarks on the Postcommunio in Some Reformed Liturgies," in *The Sacrifice of Praise,* ed. Bryan D. Spinks (Rome: Edizioni Liturgiche, 1981); Leigh Eric Schmidt, *Holy Fairs: Scottish Communions and American Revivals in the Early Modern Period* (Princeton, NJ: Princeton University Press, 1989), pp. 98-99; Millar Patrick, *Four Centuries of Scottish Psalmody* (London: Oxford University Press, 1949).

Church has an assigned communion antiphon drawn from the Psalms for every Mass.

Benedictions	Psalms 67, 115:12-15, 128
Baptism Services	Psalms 23, 42, 89, 105
Marriage Services	Psalm 8, 67, 128, 145
Healing Services	Psalms 23, 27, 121, 139 (and many more)
Funerals	Psalms 23, 46, 90, 103, 116, 121, 130, 139
Dedication of a Church Building	Psalm 84
Ordination	Psalms 117, 132, 134
Morning Prayer	Psalms 5, 30, 90
Evening Prayer	Psalms 4, 141

In each case, these choices can be either read or sung. In congregations with a fixed liturgy (perhaps governed by a prayer book), the best way to incorporate Psalmody throughout the service may be through the singing of metrical Psalms in place of a hymn (indeed, most worshipers may not be able to discern the difference between a hymn and metrical Psalm).

Homiletical Criteria

Choosing a Psalm for liturgical use can also be driven by the process of preparing for preaching. The Psalms not only help worshipers pray; they also help preachers preach.[15]

Effective use of the Psalms homiletically often involves the pairing of

---

15. See, especially, J. Clinton McCann Jr. and James C. Howell, *Preaching the Psalms* (Nashville: Abingdon Press, 2001). See also Sidney Greidanus, *Preaching Christ from the Old Testament: A Contemporary Hermeneutic Method* (Grand Rapids: Eerdmans, 1999); Thomas G. Long, *Preaching and the Literary Forms of the Bible* (Philadelphia: Fortress Press, 1993), ch. 3; Elizabeth Achtemeier, "Preaching the Praises and Laments," *Calvin Theological Journal* 36 (April 2001): 103-14.

Psalm texts with other portions of Scripture. Ellen Davis makes this point from the perspective of preaching a Psalm: "The Psalms have nearly inexhaustible potential for making connections with the larger story."[16] She invites preachers, once they have chosen a Psalm as a preaching text, to imagine that Psalm contextualized in a variety of narrative contexts — both in Scripture and in present-day life. A Psalm of deliverance (e.g., Psalm 30) might be juxtaposed both with an Old Testament healing narrative and with a contemporary situation. Preaching on Psalms often drives the preacher to other parts of Scripture.

The reverse is also true. In working with preaching texts *not* from the Psalms, it is often instructive to ask and imagine what biblical Psalms could be fruitfully juxtaposed with the chosen text. Having the freedom to explore choices far beyond the lectionary creates many interesting possibilities.

For sermons on Old Testament texts, the possibilities are endless. Consider first the evocative superscriptions that appear before some Psalms. Whatever we might feel about when those superscriptions were written and by whom, some very ancient source perceived a degree of fittingness between the Psalm and that particular event. It is not unreasonable for us to at least explore the same.[17] A sermon on David and Bathsheba is immeasurably enriched by the liturgical use of Psalm 51. A sermon on David and Absalom suggests the use of Psalm 3. Singing or reading these Psalms in conjunction with the primary Scripture text for the sermon allows the worshiper to live into the drama of a particular biblical narrative, and provides the preacher with additional material for the development of the sermon.

At times the thematic content of a Psalm, rather than its superscription, might suggest the pairing of that Psalm with a particular Old Testament event: Psalm 20 is a prayer prior to battle; Psalm 21 is a prayer after victory; Psalm 44 is a cry for help after defeat. Together they provide an option for any sermonic

16. Ellen Davis, *Wondrous Depth* (Louisville: Westminster John Knox, 2005), p. 28.

17. Erik Haglund, *Historical Motifs in the Psalms* (Stockholm: Liber Tryck, 1984). Concerning superscriptions, Patrick D. Miller comments, "While they may not be read to justify the precise situation in which the prayer was first composed, they indicate how the community of faith and those responsible for the transmission of these prayers associated them with varying human predicaments, primarily in the life of David." *They Cried to the Lord* (Minneapolis: Fortress, 1994), p. 83. Miller also suggests that we may reasonably assume that the types of laments that we know were offered by Hannah and Tamar, for example, likely correspond to the Psalms (p. 85). It is on this same basis that I am proposing the choice of Psalms for liturgical use.

treatment of the texts related to conquest or deliverance. Psalms 105, 106, and 107 are obvious correlates for any sermon on the Exodus, the desert wanderings, and the conquest of the land of Israel. A sermon on Israel's exile and return calls for the use of either Psalm 126 or 137.

A connection, though less tight, can also be made between Psalms and Old Testament prayer reports. Throughout the Old Testament, we find accounts of various persons praying to the Lord without any indication of the words they used. Think, for example, of Hannah's urgent prayers for help (1 Sam. 1:10). As Patrick Miller asserts, we may imagine "without much fear of contradiction" that such prayers for help resemble those recorded in the Psalms.[18] Choosing fitting Psalms in conjunction with these biblical texts allows the worshiper not just to hear about but to imagine more fruitfully the experience of these biblical characters.

There are also obvious pairings between specific Old Testament texts and Psalms on the basis of theological correspondence. A sermon on the covenant theology of Deuteronomy is aptly complemented by the use of a salvation history Psalm (136) or one of the Torah Psalms (1, 19, 119).[19] A sermon on the eschatological longings of the prophets is well-complemented by Psalms of Zion (46, 48, 76, 87) or Psalms of the future reign of God (96, 97). A sermon on Proverbs or Ecclesiastes is well complemented by the use of wisdom Psalms (1, 37, 49). There are easy choices for sermons on creation (8, 29, 104), sin (32, 51), and redemption (78, 105, 106). In sum, nearly every Old Testament text suggests specific points of correspondence with one or more Psalms.

For sermons on New Testament texts, the possibilities are equally numerous. An obvious connection exists in the many New Testament texts that quote Psalms. A sermon on Hebrews 1 would be well complemented by singing any of the Psalms that are quoted in that chapter. Singing the entire Psalm that is quoted allows the congregation to experience the continuity between testaments and to sense the particular way in which the ancient text was adapted for the New Testament author's use, provided that some explanation is offered in the sermon itself or in some other forum.

In addition, there is the long tradition of reading much of the Psalter

18. See Miller, *They Cried to the Lord,* pp. 84-85.
19. See Miller, *They Cried to the Lord,* p. 114.

Christologically, especially in patristic interpretations on the Psalms. The New Testament itself treats Psalms 2, 22, 69, 72, and 110 as key texts for understanding the person and work of Jesus (see Luke 24:44).[20] Other texts provide theological correlates with aspects of New Testament theology. Claus Westermann, for example, sees the theme of divine accommodation recorded in Psalms 113 and 138 as the context by which the New Testament explores the theological significance of the Incarnation.[21] And Dietrich Bonhoeffer went so far as to conclude that, "if we want to read and to pray the prayers of the Bible and especially the Psalms, therefore, we must not ask first what they have to do with us, but what they have to do with Jesus Christ. . . . The Psalms are given to us to this end, that we may learn to pray them in the name of Jesus Christ."[22] Much of modern biblical scholarship has backed off from Christological interpretations, noting the strained Christological links sometimes imagined by interpreters. In general, each Psalm can stand on its own as a prayer of the ancient people of Israel. At the same time, some Psalms take on new significance in light of the life, prayers, death, and resurrection of Jesus.

Then there are also Psalms that, together with New Testament counterparts, create evocative symbolic portraits that depict the mystery of God's grace. Consider choosing a Psalm because its central images or metaphorical

20. See Jean Danielou, S.J., *The Bible and the Liturgy* (Notre Dame, IN: University of Notre Dame Press, 1956), pp. 177-90, 311-47, with copious references to messianic interpretation of the Psalms in patristic literature and liturgical practice. See also Brian McNeil, *Christ in the Psalms* (New York: Paulist Press, 1980); Hans Joachim Kraus, "The Psalms in the New Testament," *Theology of the Psalms*, trans. Keith Crim (Minneapolis: Augsburg, 1986), pp. 177-203; T. Ernest Wilson, *The Messianic Psalms* (Neptune, NJ: Loizeaux Brothers, 1978).

21. See Claus Westermann, *The Living Psalms* (Grand Rapids: Eerdmans, 1989), pp. 297-98.

22. Dietrich Bonhoeffer, *Psalms: The Prayer Book of the Bible,* trans. James H. Burtness (Minneapolis: Augsburg, 1970), pp. 14-15. A similar view is expressed memorably in a sermon of Jonathan Edwards on Psalm 89:6: "This book of Psalms has such an exalted devotion, and such a spirit of evangelical grace every[where] breathed forth in it! Here are such exalted expressions of the gloriousness of God, and even of the excellency of Christ and his kingdom; there is so much of the gospel doctrine, grace, and spirit, breaking out and shining in it, that it seems to be carried clear above and beyond the strain and pitch of the Old Testament, and almost brought up to the New. Almost the whole book of Psalms has either a direct or indirect respect to Christ and the gospel publish. . . ." Jonathan Edwards, *Sermons and Discourses, 1720-1723,* ed. Wilson H. Kimnach (New Haven, CT: Yale University Press, 1992), p. 415.

world (e.g., military, medical, cultic) correspond with the chosen preaching text or a particular situation in the life of a given congregation.

Consider, for example, the symbolic use of water. Psalms 42:9, 69:1, and 124:3 all depict the waters of chaos that provide the symbolic matrix for the New Testament image of "drowning" (dying with Christ) in baptism. In contrast, Psalms 36:8-9, 46:4, and 87:7, along with Ezekiel 47:1-2 and Revelation 22:1-2, describe the waters that flow in Zion, the "streams which make glad the city of God." In biblical cosmology, the transformation of God's new creation is depicted in part as the transformation of the waters of chaos (Gen. 1:2) into the "sea of crystal" (Rev. 19). In worship, these images ought not merely to be explained, but experienced. Creative uses of Psalms and hymns ought to stimulate our imaginations with visions of the primeval chaos, joyful dancing streams, pillars of fire, clouds of mercy, and the multitude of other natural phenomena that are used as literary pictures to portray the vastness of God's mighty works of creation and re-creation.[23]

Given all of the ways that preachers can find correspondences between preaching texts and the Psalms, imagine a preacher or congregation who would choose to accept the discipline of ending each sermon with the reading or singing of an appropriate Psalm. Or preachers might consider identifying the key phrase in a Psalm and using it as a repeated refrain in the composition of a sermon. A sermon that includes a Psalmic refrain, "How excellent is your name in all the earth" or "why have you forsaken me?" would help worshipers sense how the ancient rhetoric of the Psalms can shape contemporary speech.[24] In this case, rather than merely serving as a response to the first lectionary reading, the Psalm would function as a response to the entire section of the service devoted to Scripture readings and sermon. This practice could relatively easily be adopted across the whole spectrum of congregations — from traditional to contemporary, "liturgical" to so-called "non-liturgical." It would work to nurture the habit of linking preaching with the life of prayer, in ways that are shaped by the biblical text.

23. It is for this reason that we might, for example, juxtapose Psalm 29 ("the voice of the Lord thunders") with the narrative of Jesus' baptism.

24. I am grateful to Debra Rienstra for this suggestion.

Pastoral Criteria

Psalms can also be chosen for use in worship for pastoral reasons. The Psalms are one of the richest resources in all of Scripture for pastoral care. What is significant for worship here is the opportunity to link the use of the Psalms in pastoral care and liturgy. Imagine a congregation marking the one-year anniversary of the death of one of its members by reading or singing a portion of the Psalm used at the funeral. Or imagine having a congregation's pastoral care leadership identify five or six Psalms as key texts for a season for use in pastoral counseling sessions, hospital and prison visits and then using those same Psalms regularly in worship (congregations that follow the lectionary might choose Psalms from upcoming lessons). This practice would connect a congregation's worship life and pastoral care ministry. And when a given Psalm is used in a home, hospital room, nursing home, or prison, the text gains a certain resonance that makes its use in worship even more pastorally significant, for both caregivers and those cared for.

One pastor I am aware of distributed various Psalm texts printed on index cards to people in the hospitals and nursing homes, leaving the cards at their bedsides for others also to read. Over time, people get exposed to many of the Psalms and can talk to the pastor about their favorites. When these loved ones die, these texts can be incorporated in their funerals and in a congregation's public worship, thus enriching the pastoral care of these people even as the deceased person is allowed to "speak" vicariously through the Psalms that they flagged as particularly meaningful.[25]

The same kind of linkage is desirable with just about every other aspect of congregational life, including ministries of education, social justice, and evangelism. Consider having each ministry of your congregation identify a particular Psalm as central to its mission. Imagine compiling the selected Psalms into a small collection that represents your congregation's ministries. Think of this as a kind of expanded mission statement — though in the form

---

25. I am grateful to Scott Hoezee for alerting me to this practice. For more on this theme, see my "How Common Worship Forms Us for Our Encounter with Death," in *Worship Seeking Understanding* (Grand Rapids: Baker Academic, 2003), pp. 291-308. For more on the Psalms in pastoral care, see Deborah van Deusen Hunsinger, *Pray without Ceasing: Revitalizing Pastoral Care* (Grand Rapids: Eerdmans, 2006), pp. 29-30, 138-46.

of scriptural poetry rather than corporate memo. Whenever the language of liturgy can echo in the resonance chamber of day-to-day congregational life, the congregation's life in ministry is enriched, and worship gains depth and force.

These examples demonstrate only some of the nearly endless possibilities for the creative juxtaposition of specific Psalms with other biblical texts. When well-chosen, the liturgical use of the Psalter has the great potential to stimulate the imaginative reception of Scriptures for worshipers in every worship tradition. For every service, there is a perfect Psalm waiting to be chosen. The goal for thoughtful worship leaders is to find it. When Egeria reported on her fourth-century pilgrimage to Jerusalem, she commented on the use of the Psalter in daily prayer at Jerusalem: "What I found most impressive about all this was that the Psalms and antiphons they use are always appropriate. . . . Everything is suitable, appropriate, and relevant to what is being done."[26] May Egeria's plaudit be a goal for all worship leaders today!

2. Choosing a Translation

Most pastors and worship leaders may not give weekly attention to the version or translation of Bible used in worship. They simply use either an officially authorized or most readily available translation. There is good wisdom in using authorized translations in worship. Regular use of authorized translations links congregations within a given Christian tradition, allows those who memorize Scripture (including children) to work with a translation they can count on being used in worship, and avoids the impression that Scripture is simply a malleable text that can be adapted as needed to suit the preferences of a given leader.

But especially given the nuance and intensity of the poetry of Psalms, there is much to be gained for leaders to be students of several translations (attempts to render the original Hebrew text in modern vernacular) and para-

---

26. Egeria, *Pilgrimage of Egeria*, XXV, trans. John Wilkinson, *Egeria's Travels* (London: SPCK, 1971), p. 126.

phrases (free compositions more or less based on the original Hebrew text). Indeed, the English language strains to capture the gritty poetic beauty of the Hebrew original.[27] We need more lyrical sensibilities, both in our reading of the Psalms and in our prayer more generally.

In other translations or paraphrases, preachers and songwriters may find a word, phrase, or image to unsettle their thoughts about a given Psalm and suggest new angles for helping modern listeners engage the text. Composers may find the cadences and rhythms of a given version more suitable for singing. Prayer leaders may choose to use a paraphrase of Scripture as a basis for a liturgical prayer, even when an authorized translation is used as the formal reading of the text.

Consider the following translations and paraphrases of Psalm 42:1-2:

As the deer longs for flowing streams,
so my soul longs for you, O God.
My soul thirsts for God, for the living God.
When shall I come and behold the face of God?   (NRSV)

As a deer stretches itself out toward the deepest, clearest spot
    of the flowing water,
that is how I stretch out myself toward you, O God —
I am thirsty for God! the living God . . .
When shall I go in and see God face to face?[28]

Like a hind crying for water,
    my soul cries for You, O God;

---

27. We should be aware that Hebrew is not only another language but comes from an entirely different family of languages. I am grateful to Nathan Bierma for his sensibilities on this point.

28. Calvin Seerveld, *Voicing God's Psalms* (Grand Rapids: Eerdmans, 2005), p. 73.

my soul thirst for God, the living God;
O when will I come to appear before God![29]

As a deer craves running water,
I thirst for you, my God;
I thirst for God,
the living God.
When will I see your face?[30]

Just as the doe longs for the springs of water,
    so my soul longs for you, O God.
My soul thirsted for the living God.
    When shall I come and appear to the face of God?[31]

A white-tailed deer drinks
    from the creek;
I want to drink God,
    deep draughts of God.
I'm thirsty for God-alive.
I wonder, "Will I ever make it —
    arrive and drink in God's presence?"[32]

29. *The Book of Psalms: A New Translation According to the Traditional Hebrew Text* (Philadelphia: Jewish Publication Society, 1972), p. 47.

30. *The Psalter*, ed. Gabe Huck, produced by the International Commission on English in the Liturgy (Chicago: Liturgy Training Publications, 1995).

31. Albert Pietersma, *A New English Translation of the Septuagint* (Oxford: Oxford University Press, 2000), p. 40.

32. Eugene Peterson, *The Message* (Colorado Springs, CO: NavPress, 1993), p. 964.

My soul thirsts for you, O God, just like a doe thirsts
    for a bubbling spring.
My soul is parched with desire for God, so vibrantly alive.
How long before I can feast my eyes on Almighty God?[33]

As a long-distance swimmer struggles towards land,
I struggle towards you, Lord.
I am in danger of drowning.
My feet long to rest on solid ground again.[34]

It is certainly true that some paraphrases of Scripture take great liberties with the Hebrew text, some in ways that genuinely help modern readers encounter the nuance of the Hebrew text, but some in ways that work directly against the central literary and theological force of the Psalm. Any innovation in word choice or sentence structure should ultimately be tested against the original Hebrew text, a task made much easier for non-Hebrew readers through any of several fine published commentaries (see the list at the end of this volume). In general, I would advocate against two extremes: on the one hand, capricious use of various paraphrases that we "raid" in order to make the text say what we want to say, and on the other, reluctance to consult anything but the authorized version for our tradition. In worship itself, one way to achieve a balance is to use an authorized version for the formal reading or singing of the Psalm, and to draw on paraphrases for use in shaping prayers, sermons, or spoken transitions.

---

33. Juanita Colón, *The Manhattan Psalter: The Lectio Divina of Sister Juanita Colón* (Collegeville, MN: Liturgical Press, 2002), p. 67.

34. James Taylor, *Everyday Psalms* (Winfield, BC: Wood Lake Books, 1995), p. 59.

Translations and Paraphrases of the Psalms

In addition to the standard Bible translations, see the following translations:

Arackal, Joseph J., V.C. *The Psalms in Inclusive Language.* Collegeville, MN: Liturgical Press, 1993.

The Book of Psalms: A New Translation according to the Traditional Hebrew Text. Philadelphia: Jewish Publication Society, 1972.

The Grail Psalter. Chicago: GIA Publications. A translation that aspires to evoke the "musical" quality of the Hebrew text, by regularizing the number of accentuated syllables in each poetic line. There have been a few subtly different editions of the Grail Psalter published in the last forty years, with another one anticipated that will incorporate the requirements of *Liturgiam Authenticam.*

The New Jerusalem Bible. Garden City, NY: Doubleday, 1985. A translation, prominent in Roman Catholic usage, that gives special attention to the literary quality of the English.

Pietersma, Albert. *A New English Translation of the Septuagint.* Oxford: Oxford University Press, 2000.

The Psalter. Gabe Huck, ed., produced by ICEL (the International Commission on English in the Liturgy). Chicago: Liturgy Training Publications, 1995. The lengthy subtitle of this work suggests its value: "A faithful and inclusive rendering from the Hebrew into contemporary English poetry intended primarily for communal song and recitation."

Psalter for Christian People: An Inclusive-Language Revision of the Psalter of the Book of Common Prayer. Gordon Lathrop and Gail Ramshaw, eds. Collegeville, MN: Liturgical Press, 1993.

Seerveld, Calvin. *Voicing God's Psalms.* Grand Rapids: Eerdmans, 2005. Offers rugged and gritty translations that recapture the force and energy of the original Hebrew texts in compelling ways.

Tanakh: A New Translation of the Holy Scriptures according to the Traditional Hebrew Text. Philadelphia: Jewish Publication Society of America, 1917.

For paraphrases or adaptations of the Psalms, see, for example:

Brandt, Leslie F. *Psalms Now.* 3rd edition. St. Louis: Concordia Publishing House, 2004.

Colón, Juanita. *The Manhattan Psalter: The Lectio Divina of Sister Juanita Colón.* Collegeville, MN: Liturgical Press, 2002.

Mitchell, Stephen. *A Book of Psalms.* New York: HarperCollins, 1993.

Peterson, Eugene. *The Message.* Colorado Springs, CO: NavPress, 1993.

Rienstra, Marchiene Vroon. *Swallow's Nest: A Feminine Reading of the Psalms.* Grand Rapids: Eerdmans, 1992.

The Saint Helena Psalter: A New Version of the Psalms in Expansive Language. New York: Church Publishing, 2004.

Taylor, James. *Everyday Psalms.* Winfield, BC: Wood Lake Books, 1995.

Among the many discussions that evaluate translations and paraphrases of the Psalter, see the following:

Bratcher, Robert G., and William D. Reyburn. *A Translator's Handbook on the Psalms.* New York: United Bible Societies, 1991.

Hunter, Alastair G. *Psalms: Old Testament Readings.* New York: Routledge, 1999, pp. 15-32.

3. THE LITURGICAL PLACEMENT OF A PSALM

For congregations with established liturgies based on historic liturgical patterns, the position of the Psalm is usually fixed. Most often in a Service of Word and Sacrament, a Psalm is sung or read after an Old Testament reading and before a New Testament reading. Short phrases from the Psalter may be used in other parts of the service, but the use of an extended passage or entire Psalm as a larger literary unit is reserved for this part of the service. In a service of Morning or Evening Prayer, one or more Psalms are read or sung near the beginning of the service.

These practices have much to commend them. They offer a regular place for Psalmody in worship and give worshipers regular exposure to a range of Psalm texts over time. These practices also convey the sense that Scripture includes not only didactic readings but also doxological poetry. There is something altogether fitting about singing at least one of the assigned Scripture selections for the day.

In liturgies of Word and Sacrament, the use of a Psalm between Old and New Testament readings can create some ambiguity (sometimes helpful, sometimes not) about whether the Psalm is functioning as a response to the first reading or as a presentation of Scripture in and of itself. As noted above, the Revised Common Lectionary features Psalms chosen primarily to serve as responses to the Old Testament text. Yet if the Psalm is to serve as the primary preaching text, it should ideally be experienced in liturgy as something that is significant in and of itself — not only as it stands in relationship to the prior reading. At minimum, a spoken or written note could explain its function as the preaching text.

Congregations who follow the patterns of traditional liturgy may often neglect other natural opportunities for using the Psalms in worship. For example, a metrical setting of a Psalm might be sung in place of a processional or recessional hymn (unless told, most congregations may not realize the difference). Additional Psalmody may be incorporated in a sequence of songs or anthems sung during the distribution of the Lord's Supper.

Congregations who do not follow a fixed liturgy have limitless possibilities for using Psalms in worship. Some of the more typical possibilities include the following:

1. If a sermon is based on a Psalm, the Psalm (like any other sermon text) could be read or sung just prior to the sermon.

2. If a sermon includes significant references to a Psalm in addition to another primary text (as suggested above), then the Psalm could be read or sung as the second Scripture lesson prior to the sermon, or read or sung as the conclusion to the sermon.

3. Psalms of praise and thanksgiving can be incorporated into a sequence of praise songs as a service begins.

4. Psalms of lament, confession, and thanksgiving can be read or sung as the introduction to one of the prayers during worship, or as the full text of the prayer.

5. A benediction Psalm (such as Psalm 67) could be read or sung as a closing blessing to worship.

6. A service could be structured entirely around a Psalm, taking time to expand on each section of a given Psalm.

4. FRAMING THE CONGREGATION'S MODE OF ENGAGEMENT

A neglected aspect of the use of the Psalms in worship is the question of how congregations are asked to engage the text. In both formal and informal, liturgical and non-liturgical services, it is not uncommon for congregations to experience a Psalm as a jumble of odd phrases and ancient geography. Outside of monastic communities, most worshipers are not Psalm-literate. We are not familiar with their nuance and typical patterns of expression.

Being intentional about introducing the meaning and purpose of a specific text can significantly deepen the congregation's level of engagement with a Psalm. A simple explanatory sentence or a brief notice in a printed or projected order of worship can accomplish a great deal unobtrusively. A more extensive introduction might be especially valuable if the congregation is not accustomed to using the Psalms. For example, Methodist pastor James Howell offered significant printed introductions during a summer sermon series on the Psalms. In a service that focused on Psalm 73, the following text appeared in the congregation's bulletin:

> Psalm 73 is one of the most eloquent, and moving, of all the Psalms. It was Martin Buber's favorite; he asked that verses 23 and 24 be inscribed on his tombstone. And the last of Charles Wesley's 6,500 hymns was written on his deathbed, and it was inspired by Psalm 73. It begins with a little motto, one of those familiar religious sayings everyone knows and loves: "Surely God is good to the pure in heart."
>
> But this Psalmist has a few questions, and they are intensely personal. Verses 1-12 are an outburst, a cry against the unfairness of life. The Psalmist, in some ways like Job, has been faithful to God — but has enjoyed no great "good" from God. Instead he has faced constant sickness and poverty, all made worse by the fact that he has to look upon wicked people who are all health and prosperity. Aren't there rewards for goodness? and punishments for wickedness? Why does it seem reversed so often? Verses 13-17 form a turning point, as the Psalmist manages not to jettison his faith in God. Somehow, going to the sanctuary of God changes everything. Verses 18-28 then form one of the most beautiful ex-

pressions of faith in God, love for God, and intimacy with God in all of the Bible.[35]

In addition, at the beginning of each season, consider printing a schedule of the Psalms that will be used each week in worship, with an invitation for worshipers to study or pray them prior to their use in worship.

Psalm Types

One of the most helpful single pieces of information for a congregation to know as it encounters a Psalm for the first time is what type of Psalm it is. Psalm scholars use a variety of terms to name particular genres of Psalms, but most groupings of the Psalms feature a list of genres such as the following:[36]

Salvation History Psalms	These are Psalms of thanksgiving for God's actions. They read like condensed history lessons about God's saving work with the people of Israel (see Psalms 78, 105, or 136).
Lament Psalms	These are texts that begin with laments to God about the brokenness and pain of life. Most laments move from expressions of anger to expressions of trust or praise (with Psalm 88 as the notable exception). Scholars often divide these texts into groups of "community laments" (such as 80, 85, or 137) and "individual laments" (such as 3, 22, or 42).

35. James C. Howell, "The Psalms in Worship and Preaching: A Report," in *Psalms and Practice,* ed. Stephen Breck Reid (Collegeville, MN: Liturgical Press, 2001), pp. 132-33.

36. These categories are highly contested among some Psalms scholars. Most introductory texts on the Psalms include a scheme for organizing Psalm types. Hermann Gunkel was an influential pioneer in studying Psalm types; see Hermann Gunkel and Joachim Begrich, *An Introduction to the Psalms: The Genres of the Religious Lyric of Israel,* trans. James D. Nogalski (Macon, GA: Mercer University Press, 1998); this work categorizes the Psalms into five major and five minor types. Sigmund Mowinckel simplifies the list into four major Psalm types: communal praise and thanksgiving, private thanksgiving, lament, and prayer; see Sigmund Mowinckel, *The Psalms in Israel's Worship,* trans. D. R. Ap-Thomas (Grand Rapids: Eerdmans, 1964, 2004). Claus Westermann simplifies the list further into two main types: praise and petition; see Westermann, *Praise and Lament in the Psalms* (Atlanta: John Knox Press, 1981).

Thanksgiving Psalms	Scholars often divide these texts into groups of "community thanksgivings" (such as 124) and "individual thanksgivings" (such as 116).
Hymns of Praise	These are texts that focus on the praise of God — usually with reference to God's being and character (in contrast to God's actions in history).
Wisdom Psalms	These Psalms are like parts of the book of Proverbs, featuring wise statements about faithful living (see Psalms 37, 49, and 133).
Torah Psalms	These Psalms both extol the virtues of God's law and summarize part of the law (see Psalms 1, 19, and 119).
Songs of Trust	These Psalms express trust as their main motif (see Psalms 11, 23, and 27).
Covenant Renewal Liturgies	These Psalms model and teach the importance of faithful, covenant (or promise-based) prayer (see Psalms 50 and 89).
Royal Psalms	These Psalms feature references to the kings of Israel and are usually interpreted by Christians in a messianic way — as referring to Jesus (see Psalms 2, 72, and 110).
Zion Psalms	These Psalms extol the virtues of Mount Zion, the location of the temple in Jerusalem, and thus focus on the beauty of the presence of God (see Psalms 46, 84, and 122).
Enthronement Psalms	These Psalms are directed to or about a king. They highlight the image of God as the ruler of creation (see Psalms 24, 47, and 95–99).
Psalms of Ascent or Pilgrim Psalms	Psalms 120–134 are those that were sung by the people on their pilgrimages to Jerusalem.

Even a simple note in a printed order of service or spoken by a Scripture reader (e.g., "hear Psalm 50 — a text for covenant renewal between God and the people") can help the congregation enter into its meaning more quickly. To be sure, the reading or singing of the Psalms in worship should not be a didactic experience with long explanations that overwhelm the beauty and power of the text. But brief introductory words can effectively highlight for worshipers the significance and central meaning of the text in unobtrusive ways.

Contemplation or Prayer

When Scripture is read in worship, the congregation is most often invited to contemplate the text. A narrative from 1 or 2 Kings, for example, invites the congregation to remember a certain historical episode and contemplate its meaning. A treatise from Paul invites the congregation to ask particular questions about the mystery of the gospel or to analyze its own level of commitment and obedience. But the texts of the Psalms are more intimate. When we invite people to read or sing a Psalm, we are placing words of prayer on their lips. We are inviting the congregation to make the prayers of the Psalms their own. The Psalms thus often engage us more personally, more intimately than other forms of biblical literature.

This raises the larger question. Are all the Psalms prayer, our speech to God? Or are they primarily Scripture, God's speech to us?[37] We can approach these questions by briefly considering Scripture as a whole. Scripture has a variety of functions in Christian worship and the life of prayer: it is the basis for proclamation, a sourcebook for meditation, a handbook for instruction, as well as a prayer book for liturgical praise and petition. The book of Philippians, for example, contains various types of texts that might be used in a variety of ways in worship: its opening greeting (1:2) might function as a liturgical greeting; its great Christological hymn (2:5-11) might serve as a text for Christian praise; its testimony about life in Christ (3:2-11) might serve as a text for expository preaching; its call to persistent prayer (4:6) might be read as a

---

37. See Davis, *Wondrous Depth*, p. 18; see also Howard Neil Wallace, *Words to God, Word from God: The Psalms in the Prayer and Preaching of the Church*, ch. 1. Christoph F. Barth argued that, although "there is no doubt that it [the Psalter] is meant to be frequently read and prayed . . . the Psalter is intended just as much, if not more, to be listened to. . . ." In part, this is important to "make clear the whole strangeness and harshness, the indelibly 'Israelite' element in the Psalms." "The Psalms in the Worship of the Church," *Introduction to the Psalms* (New York: Charles Scribner's Sons, 1966), p. 74.

biblical warrant for liturgical intercession. The same is true of the Psalms: some are typically used as prayers (e.g., 51); some as mentors for meditation (e.g., 119); some as oracles for proclamation (e.g., 50). Many Psalms function in more than one way depending on their content and their liturgical context. Consider Psalm 72, for example, which Robert Alter notes, "manages at once to be prayer, prophecy, portrait, and benediction."[38] This is why James Luther Mays speaks of the functions of praise, prayer, *and* instruction for the Psalter in the life of faith.[39] Just as in theology and in the living of the Christian life, the texts of Psalms fulfill more than one function in Christian liturgy.[40]

Consider, then, a spectrum of possibilities in which a congregation might be asked to engage with a Psalm in worship.

Praying ——————— *Meditating* ——————— *Wrestling*

On one end of the spectrum, there are (frequent) times we invite worshipers to actually pray the Psalm, to make the words of the text their own. This is the most intimate form of engagement. Congregational singing is an especially appropriate way to invite personal engagement with the text; silent prayer, perhaps interspersed with a poignant reading of the text, is another.

---

38. Robert Alter, *The Art of Biblical Poetry* (New York: Basic Books, 1985), p. 131.

39. James Luther Mays, *The Lord Reigns: A Theological Handbook to the Psalms* (Louisville: Westminster John Knox Press, 1994), pp. 20-22. The varied functions of Psalmody in early Christian worship is described by Paul F. Bradshaw, "From Word to Action: The Changing Role of Psalmody in Early Christianity," in *Like a Two-Edged Sword: The Word of God in Liturgy and History,* Essays in Honour of Canon Donald Gray, ed. Martin R. Dudley (Norwich, UK: Canterbury Press, 1995), pp. 21-38.

40. See discussion in Paul F. Bradshaw, *Two Ways of Praying* (Nashville: Abingdon Press, 1995), pp. 89-96. I believe that it is this point that provides the correct angle to address the difficult question regarding the use of the imprecatory Psalms in public worship. The imprecations cannot be used as liturgical prayer without a great deal of explanation. Yet they might function poignantly in liturgy as a source for meditation or exposition. For example, consider the striking juxtaposition of Psalmic imprecations against the enemies of God with a New Testament reading concerning the "powers and principalities." Or consider reading the imprecations in stark juxtaposition with Jesus' command to pray *for* our enemies. In both cases, the imprecations have profound liturgical possibilities, if handled with care. See also Erich Zenger, *A God of Vengeance: Understanding the Psalms of Divine Wrath* (Louisville: Westminster John Knox, 1996).

On the other end of the spectrum there are Psalm texts we don't dare pray on first reading — particularly the imprecatory Psalms. They are Psalms we struggle with. This form of engagement might be cultivated by reading the Psalm and leaving time for silent reflection. Alternatively, a worship leader might suggest what kinds of people (both within and beyond the congregation) might quite naturally pray a Psalm like this, and invite the congregation to offer the text in solidarity with them.

In between these two modes of engagement are texts that we meditate on, that we ponder, savor, and delight in. Here we want the congregation to engage and appropriate the text, but also have time to allow the text to sink in. Responsorial Psalmody (described below) is one way of rendering the Psalms that allows for this kind of engagement, with its alternation between a congregational refrain and verses sung by a solo or cantor.

Finally, it could be very appropriate for a given service to allow worshipers to engage a Psalm text in two ways. For example, in a service in which the Psalm is the basis for preaching, the sermon might aim to help a congregation move from puzzling over a Psalm to actually praying it. In this case, the Psalm could be read by a solo reader or choral reading group prior to the sermon and sung by the now-more-knowledgeable congregation after the sermon.

Christological Framings of Psalm Texts

Each Psalm text conveys different meanings in light of the person of Jesus and the teaching of the New Testament. This is especially true for messianic Psalms such as Psalms 24, 72, and 110, and Psalms that Jesus quoted, such as Psalm 22. For Psalms like these, thoughtful worship leaders have the opportunity to either highlight or downplay their Christological significance, sometimes with something as simple as a one-phrase spoken introduction.

If Psalm 22 is introduced (either verbally or in a printed service folder) with the phrase "the Psalm Jesus quoted from the cross," or if Psalm 72 is introduced with the phrase "a Psalm to extol the virtues of the king, true enough for King Solomon, even more fitting for Jesus, the Christ," the Christological frame becomes very explicit. The same effect is achieved through the use of an explicitly Christological spoken or sung refrain (see "Responsorial Psalmody" below).

Some congregations never practice such framing, leaving more to the imagination. Others always practice such framing, sometimes with elaborate teaching comments prior to the reading of any Scripture text. Perhaps a wise rule of thumb to suggest is that any introductory comments or framing like this should match the liturgical context. When a Psalm is chosen for Christological reasons, then find a simple, unobtrusive way to make that clear. When it is not, then any Christological framing notes will likely only distract or puzzle worshipers.

In either case, there is great value in moderation, offering enough information to evoke deeper understanding by worshipers, but not so much that the entire meaning of the text is pinned down before it is read. Like all effective poetry, the texts of the Psalms, with their powerful imagery and cadences, command a power all their own.

The Psalms in New Testament Context

Such framing of a Psalm through a spoken or written introduction, musical refrain, or other liturgical action can also be helpful in engaging other kinds of Psalm texts. We hear explicit Psalmic prayers against the enemy quite differently in light of Christ's command to pray *for* our enemies. One historical liturgical practice that arose, in part, out of this sense of discontinuity was the use of a brief Psalm prayer following the liturgical recitation of a Psalm. These prayers interpreted the Psalms in light of New Testament experience.[41] Thus Psalm 104, with its intriguing reference to the cosmic work of the spirit of God, could be followed by this collect:

> God of majesty, we are constantly surrounded by your gifts and touched by your grace; our words of praise do not approach the wonders of your love.

41. See texts of ancient Psalm-collects in A. Wilmart and L. Brou, *The Psalter Collects from V-VI Century Sources,* Henry Bradshaw Society, vol. 83 (London: Henry Bradshaw Society, 1949). For recent texts, see *The Book of Common Worship* (Louisville: Westminster John Knox Press, 1993), pp. 611-783. Psalm prayers were introduced to the Reformed tradition in some early metrical Psalters in both Geneva and Scotland; see J. A. Lamb, *The Psalms in Christian Worship* (London: Faith Press, 1962), p. 153.

Send forth your Holy Spirit, that came in fullness at Pentecost that our lives may be refreshed and the whole world may be renewed, in Jesus Christ our Lord. Amen.

What was implicit in the Psalm (the work of the Holy Spirit) is made explicit in the Psalm prayer. A similar effect is achieved by concluding a Psalm with the *Gloria Patri* or by following the reading of a given Psalm with a Christian hymn based on the same text. For example, follow Psalm 72 with Watts's "Jesus Shall Reign Where'er the Sun," Psalm 98 with Watts's "Joy to the World," or Psalm 46 with Luther's "A Mighty Fortress Is Our God." These three familiar hymns are all based on Psalms — but they each not only reflect but also interpret the Psalms on which they are based.

Each of these liturgical practices has subtle ways of helping worshipers sense at once both the continuity and discontinuity between the Old and New Testaments. These practices are also wonderful topics for church education Bible sessions. Many of the best church education sessions not only teach biblical literacy but help congregations better understand the use of the Bible in personal and communal worship.

5. STUDYING THE PSALM

Once we have chosen a Psalm and placed it in worship, how should we bring it to life?[42] How can we lift it off the printed page in a way that does justice to the power and poetry of the text?

Every rendering of a Psalm, whether spoken or sung, is an act of interpretation. As J. P. Fokkelman argues, "Whether they realize it or not, readers, when engaged in the act of reading, are extremely involved: they infuse a text with meaning."[43]

42. See also David Held, "The Psalms," and Paul G. Bunjes, "The Musical Carriage for the Psalms," both in *Lutheran Worship: History and Practice*, ed. Fred L. Precht (St. Louis: Concordia Publishing House, 1993), pp. 471-77.

43. J. P. Fokkelman, *Reading Biblical Poetry: An Introductory Guide* (Louisville: Westminster John Knox Press, 2001), p. 49.

Sometimes our renderings of the text fit beautifully with the text itself: imagine a reader reading Psalm 22 with quiet, somber longing, until making a transition to a brighter, even exuberant rendering of its final doxological verses (vv. 22-31).

Sometimes, however, reading can undermine the text. Reading Psalm 2 on automatic pilot — with the same tone of voice for "let us break their chains" (v. 3) and "today I have begotten you" (v. 7) — dulls the force of the contrasting rhetoric of the Psalm. Indeed, reading on automatic pilot usually induces congregations to listen on automatic pilot.

Sometimes, out of sheer necessity, someone will have to read a Psalm in worship with only a few moments of prior rehearsal. Or a musical setting of a Psalm will be chosen in which a composer has already made key decisions about how the rhetoric of the Psalm (its pace, structure, script, and poetic cadence) will be rendered. Yet one of the most rewarding disciplines for any public Scripture reader and for any liturgical musician is that of careful study of the Psalm text — to notice how the form of the Psalm and its particular words and images each convey meaning. Careful literary and theological analysis of Psalm texts can lead to profound devotional encounters with the text, and can lead to liturgical use of the texts in ways that help worshipers pray the Psalms more meaningfully.

As with most poetry, the best place to begin in encountering the text is simply to read it (out loud). As one poetry scholar put it, "A poem may turn out to be a deep and complex experience, but the experience begins by responding to the language of poetry in front of you, not by detective work that puts that response aside."[44] Reading the text out loud once a day for a week, each time trying to simply make clear what is there, generates the kinds of questions that help us encounter the text more meaningfully.

44. Kenneth Koch, *Making Your Own Days: The Pleasure of Reading and Writing Poetry* (New York: Touchstone, 1998), p. 111.

Pace

The Psalms require a sense of *pace* suitable to their content. Psalms 96, 98, 121, and 149, among others, cry out to be spoken or sung with a sense of anticipation. Their crisp imperatives and tight parallelisms — salient attributes of the Hebrew poetry that most often (but not always) come through in translation — call for use of a bright pace. One acclamation of praise propels us into the next. In contrast, Psalm 51 or 73 require deliberate solemnity. They invite worshipers to pause for moments of silent reflection.

In general, in early twenty-first-century North America, our liturgical readings and music are often too fast. One of the key characteristics of poetry is its density, the way it compresses significant meaning into a modest number of lines. In general, the best kind of exposure to poetry — even in translation — is to give it more time.

Structure

Praying the Psalms can be enriched by sensitivity to their *structure*. Consider the following examples:

Psalm 19   The genius of this Psalm lies in its stark juxtaposition of creation (vv. 1-6) and law (vv. 7-13) motifs. Even the hastiest examination of the Psalm reveals its bi-partite structure. My suggestion is to find ways to make this structure and its redolent meaning come to life through its liturgical use. Consider rendering the Psalm with two readers or cantors, each speaking one half of the Psalm (vv. 1-6, 7-13), allowing the congregation to join in the final prayer of dedication (v. 14). Or, in a congregation that does not follow a strict liturgy, allow the Psalm to inform the structure of the first two parts of a worship service, where the service might begin with the singing or reading of the first half of the Psalm along with acts of praise for creation, and then continue with the second half of the Psalm as a spur to confession and a guide for gratitude.

Psalms 34   These Psalms, similarly, both begin with the praise of God and
and 92   continue with instruction in the wisdom of God. In so doing,
they cohere with the structure of most Sunday services of the
Word. They might be used in two parts: one, at the beginning of
worship, with its typical focus on praise; the second, to precede
the Scripture readings and sermon. Alternatively, they might be
used in their entirety to pivot from the "praise" section to the
"proclamation" section of worship.

Psalm 90   This is a Psalm in three stanzas, each of which features a very different perspective on time.[45] Consider using three readers or
cantors to heighten the contrast between these three sections.

Psalm 13   The ultimate significance of this Psalm, and many other Psalms
of lament, depends on the arresting adversative "but" (v. 5) that
pivots into the final vow of praise. Something — whether a musical accent, a change in readers, cantors, gesture, tone of voice
— should highlight this key structural element.

Psalm 103   This Psalm's genius lies, in part, in the way that wise instruction is
embedded in praise. Its meaning, in part, lies in its structure. Consider introducing Psalm 103 by saying that it is like "an entire worship service wrapped up in a poem: it begins with a call to worship, continues with a medley of praise, leads up to a sermon-like
proverb, and concludes with an extended doxology."

Thoughtful composers, Scripture readers, and preachers gain much by
asking how a Psalm's structure might inform how it is to be sung, read, or
preached.

In summary, consider the structure of a Psalm as a guide for bringing the
Psalm to life in liturgy. Preachers are accustomed to outlining both their text
and their sermons. Some homileticians have argued that the outlines of the
text and the sermon should look alike most of the time. I am suggesting that
we begin to apply the same skills to liturgical practice, both for the rendering

---

45. Alter, *The Art of Biblical Poetry*, p. 129.

of Psalm texts in worship and for planning how the various elements of worship might be combined.

Script

Praying the Psalms requires sensitivity to their implicit or explicit *script*. We need to be like playwrights both as we study Psalms and as we use them liturgically. Before singing or reading a Psalm in worship, imagine scripting the Psalm for a choral reading group of four or forty people. Who should say what line — and why? As I have already described, many Psalms feature a complex juxtaposition of acclamations, petitions, oracles, and proverbs. Yet upon first reading (which is often the *only* reading for a congregation), these variations are not altogether clear.

My suggestion is that when Psalms are sung and read, worship leaders should acknowledge their script and, when possible, assign roles in the assembly that call attention to dramatic shifts in voice. Oracles of salvation should be read by a single worship leader in response to the common prayer of the congregation. The shift in voice between Psalm 32:7-8 suggests a shift in the script for how the Psalm is sung or read. Likewise, the oracle of Psalm 12:5 or Psalm 50:5, 7-15, 16b-23 might best be read or sung by a different voice than the one that begins the Psalm. The same strategy might work well with proverb-like wisdom sayings that are interspersed in the Psalms (103:15-19).[46]

More challenging are Psalms of lament, in which a salvation oracle, whether explicit or implicit, functions as a hinge that transforms a lament into an anticipation of thanksgiving. Thunderous silence cries out from between the lines of Psalm 6:7-8. Quite possibly, in the ancient temple liturgy, words of assurance or an oracle of salvation was spoken at this point.[47] In our use of the

---

46. See Robert Davidson, *Wisdom and Worship* (Philadelphia: Trinity Press, 1990), pp. 31-46. See also Joyce Zimmerman, *Pray without Ceasing: Prayer for Morning and Evening* (Collegeville, MN: Liturgical Press, 1993), which features the voicing of several Psalms for use in the context of daily prayer services, as well as helpful explanations in the introduction.

47. See Joachim Begrich, "Das priesterliche Heilsorakel," *Zeitschrift für die alttestamentliche Wissenschaft* 52 (1934): 81-92. See Miller, *They Cried to the Lord*, pp. 141-47, for more on salvation oracles.

Psalter, the very least we might do is to interpose a brief time of silence if speaking the Psalm or a brief musical interlude when singing the Psalm.

Not only do the implied speakers change, but so also does the implied audience. Psalm 30 begins with an address to God (vv. 1-3) and shifts to an address to the gathered congregation (vv. 4-5), only to return to a direct address to God (vv. 6-12). A shift in readers, or in tone of voice, or in posture or gesture can reflect this change. At times Psalmic speech is "interior dialogue," the speech of the Psalmist directed to the self (e.g., "Bless the Lord, O my soul").[48] Such phrases could be read by a single voice, with the complementary calls to praise directed to the whole cosmos read by the entire congregation. Psalm 4 may well be directed to two groups of people, the first a hostile group of enemies (vv. 2-3), the second a group of dispirited friends (vv. 4-5).[49] Again, the pacing and tone of a liturgical rendering of this Psalm might well reflect this subtle change. No Psalm has a more complex script than Psalm 2, with separate lines spoken by the kings of the nations (v. 3), the Lord (v. 6), and the one anointed by the Lord (vv. 7ff.) — see an example of Psalm 2 for choral reading on pages 89-90 below. In sum, creative liturgical usage, even to the point of scripting the Psalm, may do more for our understanding and participation in a Psalm than many expository sermons. Many congregations, even small congregations, are blessed with those skilled in dramatic arts, including junior-high drama teachers and high-school students who participate in school plays. Often these are people with talents waiting to be used to bring the Psalms to life.

Poetic Lines

Praying the Psalms is enriched by sensitivity to their poetic qualities. At the most basic level, careful study of the text begins by simply observing where each poetic line ends. Poetic lines are more important than the verse markings found in the modern biblical text.

48. The term "interior dialogue" is from Luis Alonso Schökel, *A Manual of Hebrew Poetics* (Rome: Editrice Pontificio Istituto Biblico, 1988), p. 178.
49. Schökel, *A Manual of Hebrew Poetics,* p. 197.

Indeed, responsive readings spoken directly from a printed Bible often manage to split poetic lines in ways that make even amateur poets cringe (see Psalm 19:4-5 for one example of where the verse markings do not match the natural divisions of the poetry). Instead of responsive readings, consider a choral reading of the Psalms that allows variance in pace and sensitivity to parallel structures (see descriptions below). This strategy allows each reader to express the particular nuances of his or her assigned lines. It also involves the congregation enough to sustain interest, without overwhelming them with so much text to speak that following the meaning of the text becomes impossible.

Parallelism

Parallelism is the most common and significant Hebraic poetic device. A huge portion of the Psalms feature verses that seem at first glance to say the same thing twice (such as Psalm 3:1: "O Lord, how many are my foes! How many rise up against me!"). An effective reader is almost instinctively aware of this, using the pacing and tone of the reading to convey the relationship between the two (and sometimes three) related lines.

It is important to realize, however, that parallelism is not merely an archaic poetry form resulting from the perceived need to say things twice. Rather, each slight alteration of the text helps us see a given reality in a new way — just as looking at an object with one eye and then with two eyes helps us perceive nuances and depth in an object.[50]

Parallelism also shapes the elegant rhythm and cadence of the text. It allows the text to breathe, and it conveys an expansive vision of the world. In the words of Celestin Charlier, parallelism in Hebrew poetry is "not only to enrich the primary statement by giving it precision, but also to create a gradual and insistent rhythm. The result can be compared to a succession of waves, ebbing and flowing over a rock, or to a series of concentric circles rising in a spiral around an axis."[51]

Even when an idea is presented twice in a single verse, there is usually subtle

50. Fokkelman, *Reading Biblical Poetry*, p. 78.
51. Celestin Charlier, *The Christian Approach to the Bible* (New York: Paulist Press, 1967), p. 138.

variation in the restatement that adds nuance and depth. Psalm 100:3, for example, testifies, "It is God who made us, and we are his," and then restates the point, "We are his people, the sheep of his pasture." The restatement of the theme conveys the same basic point but adds the evocative sheep-pasture metaphor. An effective reading of the text could, through subtle changes of the tone of voice and pacing, convey that those two statements are intimately related but also that the second line introduces something new and lovely to reinforce the point.

These examples are a form of parallelism known as "synonymous parallelism." But there are other forms of parallelism as well. Some verses present "antithetical" lines (such as Psalm 27:10: "Though my father and mother forsake me, the LORD will receive me"). Still other verses develop a comparison over the course of two lines, such that either line would be incomplete without the other (such as 103:11: "For as high as the heavens are above the earth, so great is his love for those who fear him").

To use a phrase from above, it is extremely tempting for readers of the Psalms to read on automatic pilot: that is, tempting to develop a regular, predictable cadence in which they read every verse in pretty much the same way, with the same falling of vocal pitch near the end of every line. Yet the nuances of the biblical text resist this. Some verses present lines that are essentially synonymous; others introduce subtle metaphors in their second line; others present stark contrasts. Learning to recognize and cherish these subtle moves is one well-tested way to come to love the Psalms more deeply. And in each case, these poetic nuances suggest ways of reading or singing the Psalm more imaginatively. After pondering the inner workings of each Psalm, it is difficult to read the text out loud in the same way again.

In these ways, rhetorical criticism of the Hebrew text teaches us not only how to exegete the text for homiletical purposes but also how to realize the Psalm in liturgy. Rhetorical criticism calls liturgical leaders to function like twenty-first-century apprentices of German baroque composer Heinrich Schütz, whose brilliant settings of the Psalms show remarkable attention to many of these same poetic nuances.

To be sure, most worshipers are not interested in which verses of a given Psalm feature antithetical parallelism. But it is equally true that worshipers *will* come to highly value the thoughtful and poignant reading or singing of a Psalm by a worship leader who took time to study the text in this way.

Worship Planning Checklist for Preachers

Once preachers have selected a Psalm for preaching, consider the following questions. Discussing these kinds of questions would be especially valuable in a meeting of a worship team, worship planning team, worship committee, or other church leadership group. These questions may need to be adapted to the particular needs of a given congregation.

1. *How will the Psalm be presented? How might it be presented differently after the sermon as opposed to before it?*

2. *What information will members of your congregation need to know before they hear or sing the Psalm for the first time?*

3. *Can part of the Psalm be incorporated into one of the spoken prayers in the service? Alternatively, can the Psalm be the pattern for an extemporaneous prayer?*

4. *Can the Psalm be sung at some point in the service? What kind of music will best capture the spirit of the Psalm?*

5. *Can portions of the Psalm be used as a call to worship or benediction?*

6. *For leaders in congregations with a flexible structure of the service: Can the service itself follow (at least in part) the structure of the Psalm?*

7. *What similar Psalms can you recommend to your congregation for their personal prayers?*

Alter, Robert. *The Art of Biblical Poetry.* New York: Basic Books, 1985.

Berlin, Adele. *The Dynamics of Biblical Parallelism.* Bloomington, IN: Indiana University Press, 1985.

Brichto, Herbert Chanan. *Toward a Grammar of Biblical Poetics: Tales of the Prophets.* New York: Oxford University Press, 1992.

Fokkelman, J. P. *Reading Biblical Poetry: An Introductory Guide.* Louisville: Westminster John Knox Press, 2001.

Hirsch, Edward. *How to Read a Poem, and Fall in Love with Poetry.* New York: Harvest Books, 1999.

Koch, Kenneth. *Making Your Own Days: The Pleasure of Reading and Writing Poetry.* New York: Touchstone, 1998.

Kugel, James K. *The Idea of Biblical Poetry: Parallelism and Its History.* New Haven: Yale University Press, 1981.

Muilenberg, James. "A Study in Hebrew Rhetoric: Repetition and Style." *Vetus Testamentum* Supplement 1 (1953): 97-111.

Schökel, Luis Alonso. *A Manual of Hebrew Poetics.* Rome: Editrice Pontificio Istituto Biblico, 1988.

Stek, John H. "The Stylistics of Hebrew Poetry." *Calvin Theological Journal* 9 (1974): 15-30.

Watson, Wilfred G. D. *Classical Hebrew Poetry: A Guide to Its Techniques.* Sheffield, UK: JSOT Press, 1984.

———. *Traditional Techniques in Classical Hebrew Verse.* Sheffield, UK: Sheffield Academic Press, 1994.

6. Realizing the Psalms: Options for Singing or Speaking

Throughout Christian history, Psalms have been presented or "performed" in liturgy in many ways, both spoken (solo voice, choral reading, or congregational responsive reading) and sung (in one of several forms of chant, in responsorial settings, metrical settings, solo or choral anthems), though the vast majority of practices in history push beyond speaking to some form of song. In recent years, the Psalms have also been sung to new settings in popular, folk, or contemporary styles of music, and depicted visually. The following paragraphs briefly describe this range of options, offer commentary on their strengths and weaknesses, and provide an annotated guide to publications and recordings of each mode of presentation.[52]

Solo Reading

The simplest form of rendering a Psalm is having it read by a single reader or lector, just as with any other Scripture reading. While appropriate for all Psalms, the use of a single reader is particularly fitting for the Psalter's most intimate texts, its personal prayers of lament and trust. In fact, congregations that practice regular corporate singing or recitation of the Psalms may benefit from occasionally diverging from this practice for certain intimate Psalms (perhaps Psalm 88 or 139).

While a solo reading is relatively simple compared with some of the more elaborate forms for reading or singing, it is by no means an easy alternative. Reading poetry is a challenging assignment. The best readings are those that are alert to a Psalm's pace, form, script, and any poetic devices that contribute to its meaning (see the previous section for more details).

PRINTED RESOURCES

Seerveld, Calvin. *Voicing God's Psalms*. Grand Rapids: Eerdmans, 2005. This volume includes a recording of the author's effective and moving readings of his own translations.
Workbook for Lectors and Gospel Readers. Chicago: Liturgy Training Publications.

52. For other categorizations of ways to render the Psalms, see Kenneth E. Williams, "Ways to Sing the Psalms," *Reformed Liturgy and Music* 18, no. 1 (1984): 12-16; *Pilot Study on a Liturgical Psalter* (Washington, DC: International Commission on English in the Liturgy, 1982); Erik Routley, *Musical Leadership in the Church* (Nashville: Abingdon Press, 1967), p. 78; and Routley, "On Using the Psalms in Worship," *Exploring the Psalms* (Philadelphia: Westminster Press, 1975).

Published annually for lectionary texts. Scripture readings are printed with helps for effective interpretation.

For general guidance in the public reading of Scripture, see:

Bartow, Charles L. *Effective Speech Communication in Leading Worship.* Nashville: Abingdon Press, 1988.

Brack, Harold A. *Effective Oral Interpretation for Religious Leaders.* Englewood Cliffs, NJ: Prentice Hall, 1964.

Childers, Jana. *Performing the Word: Preaching as Theater.* Nashville: Abingdon Press, 1998.

Jacks, G. Robert. *Getting the Word Across: Speech Communication for Pastors and Lay Leaders.* Grand Rapids: Eerdmans, 1995.

Rang, Jack C. *How to Read the Bible Aloud: Oral Interpretation of Scripture.* New York: Paulist Press, 1994.

Schmit, Clayton J. *Public Reading of Scripture: A Handbook.* Nashville: Abingdon Press, 2002.

Choral Reading

Choral readings of Psalm texts offer rich possibilities for presenting the Psalms in creative and accessible ways in many congregations. The advantages are many: multiple readers convey the communal nature of many Psalm texts; a rehearsed reading promises to capture more of the poetic nuance than unrehearsed congregational reading; and the interplay among readers is useful for capturing the dialogic nature of many Psalm texts.

The danger of this practice may be the temptation toward overly complicated renderings of a Psalm by calling attention to the innovation of the performance rather than the text, though this danger is no different from dangers that face any preacher or musician in almost any part of worship.

The best choral readings of Psalm texts are those that are developed with careful attention to the text and structure of each Psalm itself, rather than through an arbitrary assignment of parts to particular voices. Consider the following examples from Calvin Seerveld, *Voicing God's Psalms:*

Psalm 8

[Chorus begins]

1 LORD, our Lord! How wonderful is your name in all the earth!
   LORD, our Lord! How wonderful is your name in all the earth!
2 You who have set your glory in the heavens
   so that your adversaries, obstinate and vindictive enemies,
         may be stilled,
   you may now find that glory praised in the mouths of us babes
         and sucklings.

[Solo voice addresses God]

3 When I look at the night sky, the work of your finger,
   When I look at the moon and the stars, held there by your hand,
4 What are we mortal humans that you remember a man
      or a woman and pay them attention?

[Chorus thunders in answer]

5 You have made us humans almost like gods,
   crowning humanity with glory, a lordliness,
6 making us rule over the work of your hands,
   with everything put under our feet:
7 sheep and cows, wild animals of the fields,
8 birds of the heavens, fish in the waters
   and whatever other creatures prowl the deep paths of the sea —
9 O LORD, our Lord! How wonderful is your name in all the earth!
   LORD, our Lord, how wonderful is your name in all the earth!

This setting of Psalm 8 would work well with a group of almost any size. Only one solo reader is needed. The switch from the group to a solo reading and back nicely complements the text's switch from first person plural to singular to plural. And the congregation might be invited to speak the last line, as a way for worshipers to express their assent to the Psalm.

Psalm 2

The wise cantor:

1 Why do the peoples of the world rage about like madmen?
Why in the world do the different nations keep on
thinking up stupid schemes?
2 Earth kings get together "for a consultation" —
important rulers hold conferences all together
against the Lord God and against God's anointed one *(mashiach).*
These earthly rulers say:
3 "Let us smash the chains of this God that hold us down!
Let us throw off the reins of God's 'anointed one'!"

Another liturgist, perhaps a priest:

4 The One who sits enthroned in heaven begins to laugh,
my Lord mimics their foolish bluster;
5 and then God turns to them in holy anger,
stops the upstarts short with God's fierce outrage:
6 "It was I! it is I who have set up my anointed king
on Zion, my set-apart mountain."

Princely ruler taking official part in the liturgy:

7 Yes, I will recite the decisive appointment by the Lord God.
God said to me:
"You are my son. Today is the day I have borne you.
8 Ask it of me and I will give you peoples of the world
for your heritage;
the most distant nations of the earth will be yours to tend.
9 You may have to break them with a rod of iron.
You may have to smash them for remolding
as a sculpting potter reshapes her clay dish — "

[The congregation stands]

Wise cantor again:

10 So now, you small-time little rulers, you had better wise up!
   You who only judge on the earth,
   hadn't you better get the point?
11 Serve the LORD God with an attentive awe —
   Take joy *in your task only* with trembling —
   Give homage to this *adopted* son *of God too* —
   lest he also get worked up, and you obliterate any way for you to walk,
   for God's anger can flash up like lightning. . . .

Congregated chorus:

12 Blessèd are all those who have run
   to take shelter with the anointed one.
   Blessèd are all those who have run
   to take shelter with the anointed one.
   Blessèd are all those who have run
   to take shelter with the anointed one.

This example involves a bit more interpretive work, suggesting multiple readers and the dramatic element of the congregation standing. Any sermon on this text would benefit greatly from a reading that helped the congregation sense the interior drama, the shifts in voice, and the dramatic contrasts the text paints between the rulers and God's anointed.

PRINTED RESOURCES

Examples of choral readings of the Psalms can be found in:

Griggs, Donald L. *Praying and Teaching the Psalms*. Nashville: Abingdon Press, 1984.
Parker, John and Audra. *Psalms for Worship*. Shawnee Press/Harold Flammer Music.
Perry, Michael. *The Dramatized Old Testament*. Grand Rapids: Baker Books, 1994.
Seerveld, Calvin. *Voicing God's Psalms*. Grand Rapids: Eerdmans, 2005.

Responsive or Antiphonal Readings

Psalms may also be read responsively with a single leader alternating with the full assembly, or with the assembly divided into two or more groups — either by gender or by seating arrangement.[53]

Antiphonal readings are a staple of some monastic renderings of the Psalter during their cycle of daily prayer (though other monastic communities sing or chant the majority of Psalms). Responsive readings also became a prominent way of increasing congregational participation in worship among twentieth-century Protestants. A large number of twentieth-century hymnals included a section of responsive readings of the Psalms and other Scripture passages. This mode of rendering the Psalms has the advantage of being relatively easy to do with little rehearsal or preparation.

This practice is, however, very difficult to do well. And many musicians lament the lost opportunities for musical interpretation in having congregations read, rather than sing, a Psalm. Indeed, it is this practice that Earle Bennet Cross labeled as "deplorable" (see p. 15 above). There are at least three barriers to overcome to make this practice work well.

One of the barriers to effective responsive readings is the verse markings of modern Bibles, which are often used or misused to determine who reads what text. In many Psalms, verse markings do not correspond with the form or flow of the poetry (and they were added long after each of the Psalms was originally composed). This can easily be remedied by reprinting the Psalm with markers for readers that correspond to the poetic structure rather than the verse markings.

Another barrier to effective responsive readings is the low-pitched tone in which most congregations habitually read together. This is, no doubt, a difficult habit to break. But leaders could consider adding instructional cues to the reading (e.g., "read with quiet intensity" or "with urgency"), much like the composer's cues in a musical anthem. Even subtle invitations to read with interpretive sensitivity can make quite a difference in congregational reading.

Still another issue is the pace of congregational readings. Many monastic

53. Some sources make a distinction between "responsive" or "responsorial" readings (alternation between a single reader or small group of readers and the congregation) and "antiphonal" readings (alternation between two or more groups within the congregation).

communities develop over time a beautiful contemplative pace for reading the text, with ample silence between verses or half-verses. In some monastic communities, all Psalms are read at the same measured, contemplative pace, regardless of genre. This has the value of encouraging a disciplined, contemplative approach to all texts, though it does risk missing some of the exuberance of the more celebratory Psalms. Other communities intentionally develop variation in their approach to group reading, rendering Psalms of praise and thanksgiving with more exuberance and rendering Psalms of lament or intimate trust with more reflection. For congregations who use responsive reading infrequently, it can be enormously helpful to have the choir or other leadership group rehearse the reading of the Psalm ahead of time and lead the congregation in speaking their parts.

READINGS WITH MUSICAL REFRAINS

The following hymnals include several Psalms set for responsive reading, with boldface print to indicate the congregation's part. Each of the sources alternates parts between leader and people in ways that follow the poetic structure of the Psalm rather than verse divisions.

Chalice Hymnal. St. Louis: Chalice Press, 1995. Pp. 726-68.

Come, Let Us Worship: The Korean-English Presbyterian Hymnal and Service Book. Louisville: Geneva Press, 2001. In both Korean and English. Pp. 393-537.

The Covenant Hymnal: A Worshipbook. Chicago: Covenant Publications, 1996. Pp. 779-861.

Sing! A New Creation. Grand Rapids: Faith Alive, 2002. A publication of the Reformed Church in America, the Christian Reformed Church, and the Calvin Institute of Christian Worship.

United Methodist Hymnal. Nashville: United Methodist Publishing House, 1989. The official denominational hymnal of the United Methodist Church; includes 100 responsorial selections, including one for each Psalm appointed by the 1983 Common Lectionary. Pp. 736-862.

Voices United. Etobicoke, ON: United Church Publishing House, 1996. The denominational hymnal of the United Church of Canada. Pp. 724-875. (This section also includes a few metrical Psalm settings.)

Hymnal: A Worshipbook. Brethren Press, Faith and Life Press, Mennonite Publishing House, 1992. A hymnal for the Church of the Brethren, the General Conference Mennonite Church, and the Mennonite Church in North America. Numbers 811-25.

Trinity Hymnal. Atlanta: Great Commission Publications, 1990. The hymnal of the Presbyterian Church in America and the Orthodox Presbyterian Church; responsive readings for portions of most Psalms. Pp. 785-841.

Voices in Worship: Hymns of the Christian Life. Christian Publications, Inc., 2003. A hymnal for Christian and Missionary Alliance congregations; includes over 60 responsive readings based on representative examples of each type of Psalm. Pp. 674-734.

Classification Challenges

Any classification system for types of Psalm singing will be inadequate to convey the multiple possibilities that composers and songwriters have at their disposal. I have chosen to present this material in four basic categories: chant, responsorial settings, metrical psalmody, and Scripture choruses.

The challenge is that some chant involves responses by the congregation, some responsorial settings use verses that are metrical, and some metrical psalms are done in a popular music style and thus are known as Scripture choruses. Indeed, strictly speaking, the term "chant" refers, in practice, to a melodic style; "responsorial" refers to a type of leadership; "metrical" to a type of textual adaptation; and "chorus" (often) to a style of music.

Still, these four categories seem to me to map the territory most efficiently, reflecting the basic primary musical literatures used in the majority of North American congregations. My thanks to all readers for their patience in negotiating these challenges.

Chant

While reading Psalms is accessible and open to several creative variations, the vast majority of resources for rendering the Psalms in worship involve singing. The Psalms cry out to be sung. Indeed, the Psalms have been sung for three thousand years — in innumerable musical idioms and styles. The most ancient traditions for Psalm singing — and indeed, some of the most vital living traditions — involve some form of chant. Rendering a Psalm by means of chant has two main advantages. First, it invites the participation of the community (either a choir or the entire congregation), a fitting mode of expression for corporate prayer. Second, in contrast to metrical Psalmody (see below), it allows for singing the unadapted text of the Psalm.

For congregations new to chanting, the process of learning to chant together in a manageable unison may seem daunting. However, the practice is very learnable, provided there is a confident and patient musical leader. In fact, Erik Routley once referred to chant as "the only really simple way of singing [the Psalms] congregationally."[54] Over the past decade, I have been gratefully surprised to hear numerous testimonies of pastors, musicians, and worshipers in a variety of traditions who have said, in effect, "Chanting Psalmody seemed daunting, but wasn't. Once we started, it grew and developed quite naturally, and now seems as natural as breathing." Typically, the most successful chanting happens in communities with a small group or choir that rehearses it first in order to unify the pace and strengthen the basic cadences of the chant.

There are several vibrant living traditions for chanting the Psalms. Each of the following forms of chant can be rendered in several ways:

- Having the whole congregation sing the entirety of the Psalm text.
- Having a cantor (or small ensemble) sing a verse, with the entire congregation answering with the subsequent verse. This may be known as the "responsorial" form of chant (though the term "responsorial" can mean different things in the context of Psalmody).
- Having the congregation divide into two equal groups and singing each verse or half-verse in alternation. This is often called "antiphonal chant."

54. Routley, *Musical Leadership in the Church*, p. 67.

Testimony

Thomas Day's stinging criticism of post–Vatican II liturgical music in the Catholic Church is well known. In this context, his discovery of vital Psalm singing is all the more surprising. The lessons he draws from it are instructive for all leaders of the people's song.

I once visited a thriving suburban church and I was not at all surprised to come across, once again, that struggling-invalid singing so common in Catholic parishes. But at one brief point, the Responsorial Psalm, the whole church seemed to light up with singing; the booming sound of the congregation was astonishing. Afterwards, I asked the organist to reveal the secret of her success. She told me that she took a simple melodic formula that she thought was Anglican plainsong and, for most of the year, used it as the congregation's refrain at the Responsorial. The words changed from week to week but the congregation heard the same melodic idea. After a while, this melody became like a comfortable old shoe. Some in the congregation were under the false impression that they were singing an ancient chant of the church.

The common ingredients in these "success stories" are subtle: This music — special, distinctive — evoked a sense of *pride in ownership.* The singing had *effortless quality;* without displaying any hint of being self-conscious, the music flowed easily into and out of the ceremony. The music seemed to be *part of the ritual* and not something irrelevant added just to keep everyone busy. There was *no coercion* ("Now we are all going to sing this hymn and you better participate"). The melodies *sounded important,* as if they had existed forever. They were *familiar* tunes which had been *memorized.* Perhaps the inner secret of this "success" was that the music just seemed to *take place;* it did not sound like something presented to the congregation.

Thomas Day, *Why Catholics Can't Sing:*
The Culture of Catholicism and the Triumph of Bad Taste

Note that some Psalm traditions suggest alternating between a cantor and the assembly at the half-verse, with the congregation essentially completing the thought of the cantor. While this is technically possible, it also can break up the Psalm into too many tiny parts. It also can make it difficult to interpret the nuance of the poetic parallelism contained within the verse (see the discussion on parallelism above). In every form, what distinguishes chant from other musical forms is the closeness of the music to human speech. Chant is a form of heightened speech. Erik Routley once advised thinking of chant as "reading-plus" rather than "music-minus."

The following analysis describes several forms of chant: Psalm tones with pointed text, Anglican chant, Gelineau psalmody, and plainchant.

Psalm Tones and Pointed Text

The simplest form involves the use of an eight-note Psalm tone, with "pointing" marks included in the printed text.

MUSIC

The eight notes outline a simple melodic pattern that can be applied to any text, regardless of its length. Typically, the eight notes are divided into two four-note sequences, the second of which feels like a satisfying musical completion of the first. (Or, to use slightly more technical terminology: the first is an antecedent phrase; the second is a consequent phrase.)

In each of these four-note sequences, the first pitch (called the "reciting tone") is the pitch on which the first several words of each half-verse are sung. The final three notes create musical movement near the end of the phrase. Several liturgical resources offer double tones with four (rather than two) four-note clusters. These provide music for two rather than one Psalm verse.

POINTED TEXT

Printing marks included within the Psalm text itself guide singers in mapping these musical phrases appropriately onto texts — no matter how short or long a given verse might be. Each verse is divided into two parts, typically marked by an asterisk (*), with the first half of the verse sung to the first part of the Psalm tone, the second half sung to the second part of the Psalm tone. A simple mark, usually a dot, is placed above the syllable where the singer switches from the reciting tone to the remaining pitches.

Singers recite the first syllables of a line on the first pitch of the Psalm tone and then sing the last three syllables on the last three notes of the tone. The point, then, tells the singer when to change pitch. The point is usually placed above an accented syllable and at a point in the phrase that guarantees that an accented syllable is sung on the final pitch. The most effective chant is usually very much like speech. The pace for chanting a text is similar to that of reading it out loud. Accented syllables are stressed in singing, just as they quite naturally are in speaking.

Fortunately, most congregations can learn this form of chanting without any technical knowledge of textual accent, antecedent and consequent phrases, and text points. They simply hear it done, and they follow the lead.

See the following resources for this form of Psalmody:

Evangelical Lutheran Worship. Minneapolis: Augsburg Publishing House, 2006. The new official hymnal and worship book of the Evangelical Lutheran Church in America.

Lutheran Book of Worship. Minneapolis: Augsburg Publishing House, 1978. The official hymnal of the Evangelical Lutheran Church in America; includes pointed text for the entire Psalter (pp. 215-89) and ten Psalm tones (p. 291).

Lutheran Worship. St. Louis: Concordia Publishing House, 1982. Pp. 313-68. The official hymnal of the Lutheran Church–Missouri Synod. Includes the pointed text for the entire Psalter, ten Psalm tones, and instructions on chanting Psalmody.

A New Hymnal for Churches and Schools. Jeffery Rowthorn and Russell Schulz-Widmar, eds. New Haven, CT: Yale University Press, 1992. Five Psalm tones and eight antiphons, along with the pointed printing of a majority of Psalm texts (also includes thirteen metrical Psalms and twenty-four hymns based on Psalms).

Hymns and Psalms. London: Methodist Publishing House, 1983. A project of the British Methodist Conference; includes the melody line only for several chant settings of the Psalms.

Libro de Liturgia y Cántico. Minneapolis: Augsburg Fortress, 1998. Pp. 151-79. A

Spanish-language hymnal of the Evangelical Lutheran Church in America; includes pointed text for several Psalms in Spanish and multiple Psalm tones.

Rotermund, D. *Intonations and Alternative Accompaniments for LBW Psalm Tones.* St. Louis: Concordia Publishing House.

Anglican Chant

Anglican chant uses Psalm tones and a pointed text, just as in the previous example, but features Psalm tones with four-part harmony. The use of this harmony, often with organ accompaniment, has created a very expressive and beautiful form of Psalmody.

The best examples of Anglican chant feature the sensitive adaptation of a given Psalm tone to the meaning of each verse of text. Expressive organists, for example, may accompany Psalm 23 with soft and subtle sounds to accompany the words "The LORD is my shepherd," dark and brooding sounds to accompany "the valley of the shadow of death," and triumphant sounds to accompany "I will dwell in the house of the LORD forever." Expressive choir directors may, for example, ask singers to sing Psalm 24 with both quiet intensity (for phrases such as "who shall ascend the hill of the LORD") and majestic breadth (for phrases such as "The LORD, mighty in battle, is the king of glory.") The combination of a repeated harmonized melody with dramatic possibilities for choir and organ makes this form of Psalmody one of the most expressive. I should also note that some congregations have explored how this same approach to Psalmody might work with jazz chords in a very different musical idiom from the choirs and organs of English cathedrals.

MUSIC

The Anglican Chant Psalter. Edited by Alec Wyton. New York: Church Publishing, 1987.

Hymnal 1982: Service Music. Accompaniment Edition. Volume 1. New York: Church Publishing, 1982, nos. S 408-445.

The RSCM Chant Book. Croydon, UK: The Royal School of Church Music, n.d.

The beauty and popularity of Anglican chant is signaled by the significant number of available recordings.

Psalms. 2 volumes. Westminster Abbey Choir, Martin Neary, director. Virgin Classics.

The Psalms of David. 10 volumes. Priory.

Psalms from St. Paul's. 11 volumes. Hyperion.

The Psalms of David from King's Choir of King's College. 3 volumes. EMI Records Ltd.

In general, this form of chant is best for choirs and organists with ample rehearsal time. As Erik Routley once said of it: "Never was there such exquisite Psalm singing as one can count on in the cathedrals: but the congregation at large has to some extent lost this."[55] This form of chant is also very valuable for devotional use made possible by modern recordings.

Gelineau Psalmody

Eager to promote a form of chanted Psalmody appropriate for congregational use, Roman Catholic liturgical reformer Joseph P. Gelineau developed in the early 1950s a form of chant in which a regular pulse is maintained and accented syllables in the text are sung to correspond with the recurring pulse. The basic idea behind Gelineau chant, therefore, is that the presence of a regular pulse makes it easier for a congregation to sing together. This form of Psalmody was created for the French Bible, and in English it is especially associated with the Grail Psalter, a translation that gives particular attention to the pattern of syllabic stress in the English text.

When well led, this form of chant can be effective for encouraging participation; when poorly led, it can risk artificial imposition of a rhythm on a text that may be too complex to fit it. Published settings of Gelineau Psalms also feature antiphons that recur throughout the Psalm. Note that Gelineau chants

---

55. Erik Routley, *Twentieth Century Church Music* (New York: Oxford University Press, 1964), p. 108.

are most often sung with a congregational refrain — and thus could well have been included below in the section on responsorial psalmody. I have included them here because of their unique approach to chanting the text.

Carroll, J. Robert. *A Guide to Gelineau Psalmody.* Chicago: GIA Publications. A how-to guide for singing Psalms in this style.

Lectionary Psalms: Grail/Gelineau. Chicago: GIA Publications. Each Psalm in the lectionary in Gelineau-style settings. GIA also publishes several smaller volumes of Gelineau settings and a few individual Psalms. These individual settings would be useful for a choir that might experiment with this style of chanting for a particular service.

RECORDING

Joseph Gelineau: Psalms of David. With the Cathedral Singers, Richard Proulx, conductor. Chicago: GIA Publications, 1995.

Plainchant

Many plainchant settings are essentially a variation on the first one above, but with a more extensive pattern of notes to end each Psalmtone sequence. More complex patterns of chant involve use of a unique chant-like melody for each Psalm verse. Published and recording examples offer historic melodies that date back into the medieval period, from both Western and Eastern liturgical rites. The most complex forms of chant, in which the cantor improvises a melody in the style of a given chant, are often called "cantillation."

PRINTED RESOURCES

By Flowing Waters: Chant for the Liturgy. A Collection of Unaccompanied Song for Assemblies, Cantors, and Choirs. Edited by Paul F. Ford. Includes 102 Psalms. Collegeville, MN: Liturgical Press.

Hymnal 1982: Service Music. Accompaniment Edition. Volume 1. New York: Church Publishing, 1982, no. S 446.

The Plainchant Psalter. Edited by James Litton. New York: Church Hymnal Corporation, 1988. Includes a substantial introduction on the practice of chanting the Psalms; also includes plainchant Psalmtones, with pointed text, for all 150 Psalms.

Psalterium monasticum. Chicago: GIA Publications. Includes Gregorian settings of the Psalms in the Liturgy of the Hours based on the Vatican-approved *Thesaurus liturgiae horarum monasticae.*

Responsorial Psalmody (or Psalmody with Congregational Refrains or Antiphons)

The term "responsorial Psalmody" refers to any rendering of Psalms in a back-and-forth, call and response format between a leader or small group of singers and the congregation. Often, however, the term "responsorial Psalmody" has come to be associated with the use of a congregational sung refrain or antiphon in conjunction with either the reading or singing of the entire Psalm by a single voice (reader or cantor) or choir.

As they frame the Psalm text, these refrains play a significant interpretive role: they signal to the congregation a key theme or image in the text.[56] Often a key phrase or central verse of the Psalm is chosen as the antiphon or refrain. Some published settings choose refrains or antiphons that are not directly from the Psalm, but rather come from the season of the year or place in the service in which the Psalm might be sung. (Note that in some contexts the term "refrain" refers to the use of an actual line from the Psalm, while the term "antiphon" refers to a paraphrase or summary of the meaning of the Psalm.)

This form of Psalmody works especially well for Psalms that themselves have refrains, as is the case in Psalms 42, 46, 59, 80, 107, and 136, for example. It is especially effective in Psalms where a refrain may not be noticed on first reading, as in the acclamation "God is holy" in Psalm 99:3, 5, 9.

This method of Psalm singing is useful because it is easy for congregations. The congregation only needs to learn one musical phrase, while the more challenging rendering of the Psalm text is handled by a soloist, cantor, or

56. See J. Michael McMahon, *Singing Our Worship: A Pastoral Musician's Guide to the General Instruction of the Roman Missal 2000* (Silver Spring, MD: NPM Publications, 2003), pp. 12-14.

choir. This method is also valuable because it can be particularly responsive to local needs and cultural contexts. Refrains could presumably be drawn from *any* musical style; published refrains are currently available in classical, jazz, folk, folk-rock, gospel, and other musical idioms.

This method of Psalm singing has also achieved an impressive ecumenical reach in the past two generations. Several mainline Protestant, Roman Catholic, and even some evangelical publishers have issued extensive publications of responsorial Psalmody. Evangelical and Charismatic churches may well be drawn to this tradition because of the recent publication of volumes of responsorial Psalmody in a variety of folk music styles. In fact, several praise choruses (which are often based on a single Psalm verse) may be used as a congregational refrain before, during, and after the reading of a Psalm.

Responsorial Psalmody has the advantage of using the actual text, not a poetic reworking, of the biblical text (though some responsorial Psalm settings feature reworkings of the Psalm text for solo singers or cantors). In the hands of skilled composers and cantors, responsorial Psalmody calls attention to the poetic features of the Psalter that are so carefully studied by biblical scholars. It is also quite possible for local musicians to compose Psalm refrains in ways that are attentive to local needs, making this one of the most contextual forms of Psalmody.

PRINTED RESOURCES

The Basilica Psalter: Responsorial Psalms for the Parish Church. Edited by Jay Hunstiger. Collegeville, MN: Liturgical Press.

Book of Psalms. Presbyterian Church in Canada, 1995. Responsorial settings with at least two different refrain options and Psalmtones for each of the 150 Psalms.

Daw, Carl P., Jr., and Kevin Hackett. *A Hymn Tune Psalter.* New York: Church Publishing. Book 1: Advent-Pentecost, 1998. Book 2: Sundays After Pentecost, 1999. Responsorial Psalms with antiphons derived from familiar hymn tunes, with the Psalms set in simplified Anglican chant.

Lead Me, Guide Me: The African American Catholic Hymnal. Chicago: GIA Publications, 1987. Includes over twenty responsorial Psalms, with music in African-American gospel style (nos. 499-545), plus twenty Psalmtones (nos. 546-65).

Lift Every Voice and Sing II: An African American Hymnal. New York: Church Hymnal Corporation, 1993. Includes eight responsorial Psalms, with music in African-American gospel style (pp. 273-80).

Mil Voces para Celebrar: Himnario Metodista. Edited by Raquel M. Martínez. Nashville: United Methodist Publishing House, 1996. Includes responsorial settings for the majority of Psalms in Spanish (pp. 87-140).

The New Century Psalter. Cleveland: Pilgrim Press, 1999. Responsorial settings for all 150 Psalms.

Psalms and Ritual Music. Three volumes (year A, B, C), in multiple editions. World Library Publications.

Psalms for Praise and Worship. Edited by John C. Holbert, S. T. Kimbrough Jr., and Carlton R. Young. Nashville: Abingdon Press, 1992. Pointed printing of all 150 Psalms, along with 127 musical antiphons and several Psalmtones.

Psalms for the Church Year. 10 Volumes. Chicago: GIA Publications, 1988-2002. Responsorial Psalms for cantor and congregation in a folk liturgical style.

The Psalter: Psalms and Canticles for Singing. Louisville: Westminster John Knox Press, 1993. An extensive collection of responsorial Psalms and Psalmtones in a variety of formats and styles.

Psalter for Worship. 3 volumes (Cycles A, B, C). Minneapolis: Augsburg Fortress.

Singing the Psalms. 5 volumes. Oregon Catholic Press.

This Far by Faith: An African American Resource for Worship. Minneapolis: Augsburg Fortress, 1996. Numbers 1-36. Responsorial Psalms and Psalmtones, with music, in African-American gospel style.

United Methodist Hymnal. Nashville: United Methodist Publishing House, 1989. The denominational hymnal of the United Methodist Church; includes 100 responsorial selections, including one for each Psalm that is appointed by the 1983 Common Lectionary (pp. 736-862).

JAZZ SETTINGS

Jazz Psalms — Sheet Music. Grand Rapids: Calvin College, 2004. A recording of these *Jazz Psalms* is also available from Calvin College.

Swing a New Song to the Lord: Resources for Jazz Worship. Ed. Bill Carter. Presbybop Music (visit www.presbybop.com). Includes nine Psalm settings.

Alonso, Tony, Michael Mahler, and Lori True. *As Morning Breaks and Evening Sets: Psalms, Canticles and Hymns for the Liturgy of the Hours.* Winona, MN: St. Mary's Press, 2004. Includes ten responsorial Psalm settings for cantor and congregation in a folk liturgical style. A recording of music from this collection is also available from GIA Publications.

Bolduc, Ed. *A Collection of Songs and Psalms.* World Library Publications.

Burkhardt, Michael. *Psalms for the Church Year.* MorningStar Music Publishers.

Consiglio, Cyprian, OSB. *Lord, Open My Lips: Music for the Hours.* Portland, OR: Oregon Catholic Press. Includes nine Psalm settings. A recording of music from these collections is also available from the publisher.

Cooney, Rory. *Cries of the Spirit.* 2 volumes. Portland, OR: Oregon Catholic Press. Includes responsorial Psalm settings for cantor and congregation in a folk liturgical style. A recording of music from this collection is also available from the publisher.

Cotter, Jeanne. *We Are God's People: Psalms for the Family of God.* Chicago: GIA Publications. Includes ten responsorial Psalm settings for cantor and congregation in a folk liturgical style. A recording of music from this collection is also available from GIA Publications.

Gerike, Henry V. *Psallite: Psalms Settings for the Church Year.* St. Louis: Concordia Publishing. Twenty-three Psalm settings.

Guimont, Michel. *Guimont Psalms.* Chicago: GIA Publications. A recording is available from the publisher.

———. *Lectionary Psalms.* Chicago: GIA Publications. A recording is available from the publisher.

———. *Psalms for the Revised Common Lectionary.* Chicago: GIA Publications. A recording is available from the publisher.

Haas, David. *Light and Peace: Morning Praise and Evensong.* Chicago: GIA Publications. Includes four responsorial Psalm settings for cantor and congregation in a folk liturgical style. A recording of music from this collection is also available from GIA Publications.

Hawthorne, Robert A. *Portland Psalter. Book One: Liturgical Years ABC.* Church Publishing. Settings for all Psalms appointed for the Sunday Eucharist according to the Book of Common Prayer lectionary and the Revised Common Lectionary. *Book Two* contains the balance of Psalm settings as well as a CD-ROM with printable versions of the congregational refrains.

Hopson, Hal. *18 Psalms for the Church Year.* Hope Publishing Company. See also his *Psalm Refrains and Tones* and *10 More Psalms,* also published by Hope Publishing.

Hruby, Dolores. *Seasonal Psalms for Children.* World Library Publications.

Hurd, Bob, Eleazar Cortés, Jaime Cortez, Mary Frances Reza, and Donna Peña. *Cantaré Eternamente/For Ever I Will Sing: Bilingual Psalms for the Liturgical Year.* 2 volumes. Portland, OR: Oregon Catholic Press. Includes forty-six bilingual Psalms. A recording of music from these collections is also available from the publisher.

Kelly, Columba, OSB. *Lectionary Psalms for Lent and Easter* and *Lectionary Psalms for Advent and Christmas.* Chicago: GIA Publications. For cantor, assembly, and keyboard.

Kreutz, Robert. *Psalms.* Portland, OR: Oregon Catholic Press.

Psalm Songs. 3 volumes, ed. David Ogden and Alan Smith. London: Cassell, 1998. Also published by Augsburg Fortress, 1998. Responsorial Psalms for cantor and congregation in a folk liturgical style. Also available in a one-volume *Psalm Songs: Complete Set.*

Rosas, Carlos. *¡Grita de Alegría! Salmos para el año litúrgico.* Portland, OR: Oregon Catholic Press.

Schiavone, John. *A Lectionary Psalter.* Portland, OR: Oregon Catholic Press. Psalms and Gospel Acclamations for Sundays, Solemnities and Feasts for the Three-year Lectionary Cycle.

Talbot, John Michael. *Chant from the Hermitage.* Portland, OR: Oregon Catholic Press. A recording of music from this collection is also available from the publisher.

Waddell, Chrysogonus. *Psalms for the Advent Season.* World Library Publications.

Willcock, Christopher. *Psalms for the Journey.* Collegeville, MN: Liturgical Press, 1991. Twelve responsorial Psalms for cantor or choir and congregation.

Most responsorial settings use a refrain sung by the congregation, or antiphon, interspersed with the singing of the unaltered Psalm text by a cantor or choir. Some, however, use a congregation-sung refrain, interspersed with the singing of an *adapted* Psalm text by a cantor or choir. This form has become particularly popular in recent years, with hundreds of folk-like Psalm settings emerging from Roman Catholic congregations following the Second Vatican Council. Roman Catholic publishers such as GIA Publications, Oregon Catholic Press, and World Library Publications offer hundreds of published Psalm settings for cantor and congregation. Their published hymnals also include substantial sections of Psalmody, most often with a simple, folk-like refrain or antiphon for the congregation, with adapted Psalm text set for soloist (and guitar, keyboard, or small instrumental ensemble). See, for example:

Catholic Community Hymnal. Chicago: GIA Publications, 1999. See numbers 19-48.
The Collegeville Hymnal. Collegeville, MN: Liturgical Press, 1990. Numbers 104-60.
Flor y Canto. Portland, OR: Oregon Catholic Press, 1989. Pp. 494-579 (musical refrains only).
Gather Comprehensive. Chicago: GIA Publications, 1994. Numbers 18-152.
Glory and Praise. Portland, OR: Oregon Catholic Press, 1997. Pp. 167-285.
One Faith, Una Voz. Portland, OR: Oregon Catholic Press. Includes extensive bilingual responsorial Psalms.
Ritual Song. Chicago: GIA Publications, 1996. Numbers 28-200.
Worship: A Hymnal and Service Book for Roman Catholics. 3rd edition. Chicago: GIA Publications, 1998. See numbers 24-100 for settings of the majority of Psalms, with an antiphon, Psalmtone, and Gelineau-style tone.

Musicians need access to the music leader's editions of these hymnals for complete musical accompaniments.

RECORDED EXAMPLES

Haugen, Marty. *Come, Let Us Sing for Joy.* Chicago: GIA Publications, 2000. Includes eleven responsorial Psalms for cantor and congregation in a folk liturgical style.
Sing Out! A Children's Psalter CD. World Library Publications.

PERFORMANCE SUGGESTIONS

Harmon, Kathleen. *The Ministry of Cantors.* Collegeville, MN: Liturgical Press.

Metrical Psalmody

Metrical Psalms feature poetic reworkings of the biblical text that provide regular patterns of stressed and unstressed syllables so that the Psalms can be sung to hymn tunes. Some metrical Psalms also feature rhyme.

The advantage of metrical Psalmody is the accessibility of musical settings, an advantage that was central to the sixteenth-century Protestant Reformers. Metrical Psalmody was promoted by Martin Luther "so that the Word of God even by means of song might live among the people."[57] John Calvin, who restricted church music to metrical Psalmody for the congregation, contended that "the Psalms can stimulate us to raise our hearts to God and arouse us to an ardor in invoking as well as exalting with praises the glory of his name."[58] As Emily Brink concludes, "The great strength of metrical song is the accessibility and memorable quality of patterned texts and tunes to a large gathering of untrained singers."[59]

Metrical Psalmody was the exclusive form of church music for early Reformed and Presbyterian congregations, with distinct traditions of Genevan and Scottish Psalmody. The Puritans sang Psalms as they founded new communities in what became the United States, taking with them the *Ainsworth Psalter* from Europe and publishing *The Bay Psalm Book* as one of most prominent early American publications. Isaac Watts wrote numerous metrical Psalm settings. Several of his texts include explicitly Christological references. "Jesus Shall Reign Where'er the Sun," for example, is Watts's metrical setting of Psalm 72, which explicitly names Jesus as the king referred to in that Psalm. Watts's Psalmody influenced nearly every subsequent English-language hymnal and was particularly significant in shaping the musical repertoire of many African-American denominations in the United States.[60]

Metrical Psalmody has also been practiced by several other Christian tra-

57. *Martin Luthers Werke: Kritische Gesamtausgabe,* Weimarer Ausgabe: Briefe, vol. 8, p. 220; English translation: *Luther's Works: American Edition,* ed. J. Pelikan and H. T. Lehmann (St. Louis and Philadelphia: Concordia Publishing House, 1955-86), vol. 53, p. 221.

58. "1537 Articles for the Organization of the Church," *Joannis Calvini Opera Selecta,* ed. Peter Barth, Wilhelm Niesel, and Dora Scheuner, 5 vols. (Munich: Chr. Kaiser, 1926-52), vol. 1, p. 375; English translation: *Calvin: Theological Treatises,* trans. J. K. S. Reid, Library of Christian Classics, vol. 22 (Philadelphia: Westminster Press, 1954), p. 53.

59. Emily R. Brink, "Metrical Psalmody: A Tale of Two Traditions," *Reformed Liturgy and Music* 23, no. 1 (1989): 3. For an orientation to the tunes and text of historical metrical Psalms, see Paul Westermeyer, *Let the People Sing: Hymn Tunes in Perspective* (Chicago: GIA Publications, 2005), pp. 83-122; Erik Routley, *A Panorama of Christian Hymnody,* ed. Paul A. Richardson (Chicago: GIA Publications, 2005), pp. 13-38; John D. Witvliet, "The Spirituality of the Psalter in Calvin's Geneva," in *Worship Seeking Understanding* (Grand Rapids: Baker Academic, 2003), pp. 203-30.

60. Gilbert I. Bond, "Psalms in a Contemporary African American Church," in *Psalms in Community: Jewish and Christian Textual, Liturgical, and Artistic Traditions,* ed. Harold W. Attridge and Margot E. Fassler (Atlanta: Society of Biblical Literature, 2003), pp. 313-23.

ditions. In the late nineteenth century, C. P. Jones, an early African-American Pentecostal Holiness Bishop, produced several metrical Psalms for use by his congregation in Jackson, Mississippi. In the 1970s, several renewal groups began to produce metrical Psalms that could be sung to a variety of musical idioms shaped by more popular music. The Iona Community has produced a particularly influential collection of metrical psalms. Metrical Psalmody is also specifically named as one authorized form of congregational participation in the opening rites of Roman Catholic worship.[61]

Metrical Psalms vary widely in terms of how closely they correspond with the biblical text.[62] Some closely follow the logic, script, imagery, and even the parallelism of the Psalm text, while others exercise great freedom in rearranging the basic ideas of a given text. Some — especially settings of longer Psalms — omit several ideas, images, or petitions from a Psalm, while others "pad" the Psalm text with additional images or insights in order to fill out the desired meter.

Some well-known hymns are clearly inspired by specific Psalms, but they are sufficiently independent of those Psalms that they are usually categorized not as metrical Psalms but as hymns. These include such famous examples as "A Mighty Fortress Is Our God" (Martin Luther's hymn based on Psalm 46), "O God Our Help in Ages Past" (Isaac Watts's hymn based on Psalm 90), "Praise, My Soul, the King of Heaven" (based on Psalm 103), and "O Worship the King" (based on Psalm 104). Congregations (and hymnal editors) would do well to identify clearly the connection between the hymn and the biblical Psalm, a connection that most worshipers will otherwise miss.

The choice of meter is especially important when setting a Psalm. The building blocks for metered poetry are the patterns of accents that poets use to set the texts. The two most common patterns are iambic and trochaic. In the words of Austin Lovelace, iambic poetry (which alternates unaccented and accented syllables, beginning with the *unaccented* syllable) is "always urging the sound and sense onward to a final strong point of accent and thought," while

61. See McMahon, *Singing Our Worship,* p. 8; see also Christoph Tietze, *Hymn Introits for the Liturgical Year: The Origin and Development of the Latin Texts* (Chicago: Hillenbrand Books, 2005), pp. 100-119.

62. Henrietta Ten Harmsel, "Versifying the Psalms for Singing," *Reformed Worship* 4 (June 1987): 14-15.

trochaic poetry (which alternates unaccented and accented syllables, beginning with the *accented* syllable) "is abrupt . . . comes to the point immediately . . . commands attention . . . is decisive."[63]

Compare this iambic example, based on Psalm 23:

> "The <u>King</u> of <u>love</u> my <u>shep</u>herd <u>is</u>,
> Whose <u>good</u>ness <u>fail</u>eth <u>nev</u>er;
> I <u>noth</u>ing <u>lack</u> if <u>I</u> am <u>His</u>
> And <u>He</u> is <u>mine</u> for<u>ev</u>er."

to this trochaic one, based on Psalm 103:

> "<u>Praise</u>, my <u>soul</u>, the <u>King</u> of <u>heav</u>en.
> <u>To</u> his <u>feet</u> your <u>trib</u>ute <u>bring</u>.
> <u>Ran</u>somed, <u>healed</u>, re<u>stored</u>, for<u>giv</u>en,
> <u>Ever</u>more his <u>prais</u>es <u>sing</u>."

These patterns of accent (iambic, trochaic, and the other less common patterns of dactylic and anapestic) can be shaped into a nearly limitless number of meters, depending on how many syllables are in each line of a stanza. One of the most common meters, known as "Long Meter" (LM), features four lines per stanza of eight syllables each. In Lovelace's candid assessment, it is a meter that "lends itself readily to majestic subjects and stately treatment," but it does risk a tendency to dullness. Isaac Watts's Psalm 72 is a positive example:

> Jesus shall reign where'er the sun
> Does its successive journeys run,
> His kingdom stretch from shore to shore,
> Till moons shall wax and wane no more.

---

63. Austin C. Lovelace, *The Anatomy of Hymnody* (Chicago: GIA Publications, 1965), p. 63. Lovelace also adds a brief instructive comment on less common accent patterns and various rhyme schemes.

The most pervasive example in Western hymnody, Common Meter (CM), is comprised of four lines of text, the first and third with eight syllables, and the second and fourth with six (86 86). Lovelace calls this "the workhorse of hymnody," noting that it allows for simple and direct expression, especially appropriate for "teaching and conveying facts," but also that it is a "treacherously and deceptively easy meter for poets to use," which risks "monotony or flippancy" — and indeed can too easily be paired with sing-songy music.[64] A positive example of this meter is a familiar setting of Psalm 23:

> The Lord's my shepherd; I'll not want.
> He makes me down to lie
> In pastures green; he leadeth me
> The quiet waters by.

As Lovelace notes, this 1787 text creates a gentle feel by ending each line on an unaccented syllable.

In contrast to the English and Scottish traditions of Psalmody in which nearly all Psalms were set in a ballad-like Common Meter (86 86), the Genevan Psalter used 110 different meters to set 150 Psalms! Some Genevan Psalms were set in idiosyncratic meters: Psalm 81 was set to 56 55 56, with short poetic lines that create a kind of imperative intensity and breathlessness. Psalm 43 was set to 98 99 86, with long lines that yearn for the same kind of repose as the content of the text. These brief examples hardly scratch the surface of the craft of setting the Psalms in meter. The best metrical Psalms rely on a host of evocative and subtle poetic devices to help singers engage the text in ways that are at once simple and also profound.

In recent years, metrical Psalmody continues to be the exclusive form of church music for some Presbyterian denominations (e.g., the Reformed Presbyterian Church), remains prominent in the church music of others (e.g., the Orthodox Presbyterian Church, the Christian Reformed Church, the Associate Reformed Presbyterian Church), and has witnessed renewed attention in several others (e.g., the 1990 hymnal of the Presbyterian Church USA). Numerous

---

64. Lovelace, *The Anatomy of Hymnody,* pp. 25, 35. Lovelace also offers instructive examples in a number of other common meters.

recent publications signal a modest resurgence of published metrical Psalmody. Many recently published texts and tunes may well prove to be among the most accessible and creative ever produced, though their influence depends on the intentionality of congregations.[65]

One disadvantage of metrical Psalmody is that worshipers are singing an adaptation of the text (some of which depart rather significantly from the text), rather than the Psalm itself. (While it is true that every translation is an adaptation, rearranging the sense of the text into metrical poetry involves more significant changes than other forms of psalmody outlined in this book.) For this reason, several influential voices have called even Reformed and Presbyterian congregations to move away from metrical psalmody toward responsorial settings for Psalms used as responses to the Bible readings in weekly worship (thus the separate Psalters published by the UCC and PCUSA both feature responsorial psalmody rather than metrical Psalmody). However, I would add that, even when responsorial psalms are used as responses to Scripture readings, metrical psalmody remains a rich resource for any other time that the congregation would sing hymnody, including during celebrations of the Lord's Supper.

DENOMINATIONAL HYMNALS

Book of Praise. Quebec City: Presbyterian Church in Canada, 1997. The denominational hymnal of the Presbyterian Church in Canada; includes 108 metrical Psalm settings.

Book of Praise: Anglo-Genevan Psalter. Winnipeg, MB: Premier Printing, 1984. The denominational Psalter of the Canadian Reformed Church; English-language metrical settings of all 150 Psalms for use with Genevan tunes.

The Book of Psalms for Singing. Pittsburgh: Board of Education and Publication, Re-

---

65. See Darryl G. Hart, "In the Shadow of Calvin and Watts: Twentieth-Century American Presbyterians and Their Hymnals," in *Singing the Lord's Song in a Strange Land: Hymnody in the History of North American Protestantism,* ed. Edith L. Blumhofer and Mark A. Noll (Tuscaloosa, AL: University of Alabama Press, 2004), pp. 92-121; Emily R. Brink and John D. Witvliet, "Contemporary Developments in Music in Reformed Churches Worldwide," in *Christian Worship in Reformed Churches Past and Present,* ed. Lukas Vischer (Grand Rapids: Eerdmans, 2003), pp. 324-47. This article includes a brief list of metrical psalters currently in use in the Netherlands, Hungary, Switzerland, Scotland, and Japan.

formed Presbyterian Church of North America, 1973. The denominational Psalter of the Reformed Presbyterian Church of North America.

Praise! Psalms, Hymns, and Songs for Christian Worship. Praise Trust, 2000. Includes metrical settings of each Psalm, with multiple settings of select Psalms.

Presbyterian Hymnal. Louisville: Westminster John Knox Press, 1990. The denominational hymnal of the Presbyterian Church USA. Selections 158-258 feature settings of the Psalms in multiple formats (metrical, chant, responsorial), but with a predominance of metrical. The same volume is published for ecumenical use under the title *Hymns, Psalms, and Spiritual Songs* (Westminster John Knox Press, 1990).

Psalter Hymnal. Grand Rapids: CRC Publications, 1987. The denominational hymnal of the Christian Reformed Church in North America. The collection begins with metrical settings of all 150 Psalms, and includes several dozen additional metrical Psalms scattered throughout the thematic sections of the book.

Rejoice in the Lord. Grand Rapids: Eerdmans, 1985. A denominational hymnal for the Reformed Church in America. Selections 81-143 include metrical settings of roughly one-third of the biblical Psalms.

Trinity Hymnal. Atlanta: Great Commission Publications, 1990. The hymnal of the Presbyterian Church in America and Orthodox Presbyterian Church. Includes several metrical Psalm settings scattered throughout the thematically organized sections of the hymnal.

Trinity Psalter. Presbyterian Church in America, 1994. Words-only, metrical settings of all 150 Psalms, with suggestions for use with familiar hymn tunes. Both a text-only and music edition are available from Crown and Covenant Publications. Crown and Covenant Publications also distributes the Psalters of the Reformed Presbyterian Church in Japan, the Free Church of Scotland, the Presbyterian Church of Eastern Australia, and the Irish Reformed Church.

SINGLE-AUTHOR COLLECTIONS

Anderson, Fred R. *Singing Psalms of Joy and Praise.* Philadelphia: Westminster Press, 1986. Fifty-three metrical Psalms, along with suggested tunes and brief prayers that correspond with each Psalm.

Bell, John. *Psalms of David and Songs of Mary.* Chicago: GIA Publications, 1993. Includes settings of seven Psalms; a recording of music from this collection is also available from GIA Publications.

———. *Psalms of Patience, Protest, and Praise.* Chicago: GIA Publications, 1993. A recording of music from this collection is also available from GIA Publications.

Bringle, Mary Louise. *Joy and Wonder, Love and Longing.* Chicago: GIA Publications, 2002. Includes metrical settings of Psalm 42.

Daw, Carl P., Jr. *New Psalms, Hymns, and Spiritual Songs.* Carol Stream, IL: Hope Publishing Company, 1996.

Duck, Ruth C. *Circles of Care.* Cleveland: Pilgrim Press, 1998. See pp. 1-4 for settings of Psalms 8, 23, 40, and 90.

Dudley-Smith, Timothy. *A House of Praise: Collected Hymns, 1961-2001.* New York: Oxford University Press/Hope Publishing Company, 2003. Includes forty-five metrical Psalms (pp. 131-76).

Edwards, Rusty. *As Sunshine to a Garden.* Minneapolis: Augsburg Fortress, 1999. Includes paraphrases of Psalms 47, 149, 51, 23, 122, 27, 62, 66, 30, 139, 43, 65, and 121.

Grindal, Gracia. *We Are One in Christ.* Kingston, NY: Selah Publishing Company, 1996. Includes a section of twelve Psalms.

Idle, Christopher. *Light Upon the River.* London: St. Matthias Press, 1998. Includes over sixty metrical Psalms (pp. 201-64).

Kaan, Fred. *The Only Earth We Know: Hymn Texts by Fred Kaan.* London: Stainer and Bell; Carol Stream, IL: Hope Publishing Company, 1999. See pp. 86-90 for settings of Psalms 8, 23, 92, and 130.

Leach, Richard. *Memory, Take the Hand of Hope.* Kingston, NY: Selah Publishing Company, 2000. Includes a short section of paraphrases of Psalms.

————. *Over the Waves of Words.* Kingston, NY: Selah Publishing Company, 1996. Includes a short section with paraphrases of Psalms 1, 137, 8, and 150.

Leckebusch, Martin. *The Psalms.* Kevin Mayhew Publishers, 2006. Includes metrical settings of all 150 Psalms.

Morgan, Michael. *Psalter for Christian Worship.* Louisville: Columbia Theological Seminary, Witherspoon Press, and The Office of Theology and Worship, Presbyterian Church (USA), 1999.

Perry, Michael. *Singing to God.* Carol Stream, IL: Hope Publishing Company, 1995. Includes approximately sixty Psalm paraphrases.

Quinn, James. *Praise for All Seasons: The Hymns of James Quinn, S.J.* Kingston, NY: Selah Publishing Company, 1994.

Stuempfle, Herman, Jr. *Awake Our Hearts to Praise!* Chicago: GIA Publications, 2000. Includes paraphrases of Psalms 107, 147 and 148.

————. *Redeeming the Time.* Chicago: GIA Publications, 1997. Includes paraphrases of five Psalms: 139, 138, 130, 31, and 144.

———. *Wondrous Love Has Called Us!* Chicago: GIA Publications, 2006. Includes paraphrases of Psalms 18, 133, and 148.

———. *The Word Goes Forth.* Chicago: GIA Publications, 1993. Includes paraphrases of Psalms 24, 46, 90, 107, and 148.

Webber, Christopher L. *A New Metrical Psalter.* New York: The Church Hymnal Corporation, 1986.

Vajda, Jaroslav J. *Sing Peace, Sing Gift of Peace.* St. Louis: Concordia Publishing House, 2003. Includes paraphrases of Psalms 93, 130, 111, 46, 23, and 133.

HISTORICAL

The Songs and Hymns of Isaac Watts. Reprinted by Soli Deo Gloria Publications, 1997.

The Unpublished Poetry of Charles Wesley. Edited by S. T. Kimbrough, Jr., and Oliver A. Beckerlegge. Volume 2: *The Hymns and Poems on Holy Scripture.* Nashville: Kingswood Books, 1990. See pp. 441-51 for Psalm-based examples.

See also The Hymn Society in the United States and Canada for facsimile editions of *The Bay Psalm Book* (1640) and Henry Ainsworth's *Psalter* (used in the Plymouth Colony).

RECORDED EXAMPLES

Crown and Covenant Publications also lists over a dozen other recordings of metrical Psalms by individual choirs and artists.

Korean Psalter and CD Set. Twenty CDs from the Korean *Book of Psalms for Singing;* available through Crown and Covenant Publications.

Music of the Genevan Psalter. H. Henry Meeter Center for Calvin Studies at Calvin College and Calvin Theological Seminary. Available at www.calvin.edu/worship/psalms.

Psalms. Music of the Genevan Psalter recorded by the Japan Bach Collegium, conducted by Masaaki Suzuki-sensei. Available at www.calvin.edu/worship/psalms.

Psalms of the Trinity Psalter. 2 volumes. Savannah, GA: IPC Press, 1999. Scottish Festival Singers, directed by Ian McCrorie. Available through Gothic Records.

Scottish Metrical Psalms. Northern Presbytery Choir, Reformed Presbyterian Church of Ireland, conducted by Kathleen R. Wright. Five CDs; available through Crown and Covenant Publications.

"Above all, sing spiritually. Have an eye to God in every word you sing. Aim at pleasing him more than yourself, or any other creature. In order to do this attend strictly to the sense of what you sing, and see that your heart is not carried away with the sound, but offered to God continually; so shall your singing be such as the Lord will approve here, and reward you when he cometh in the clouds of heaven."

From John Wesley's *Select Hymns*, 1761

Psalm-Based Solo and Choral Anthems, Organ and Instrumental Music

There are literally thousands of choral and solo anthems on Psalm-based texts, including famous examples from George Frederick Handel's *Messiah* ("Lift Up Your Heads," based on Psalm 24) and Johannes Brahms's *A German Requiem* ("How Lovely Are Your Dwellings," based on Psalm 84). The catalog of nearly every publisher of sacred and liturgical music includes many selections based on particular Psalms, with dozens of new published Psalm settings added every year.

Many Psalm settings for solo or choir are written in what musicians call a "through-composed" form. This means that unique music is written for every phrase in the entire Psalm, without the repetition of a melody as in a hymn or responsorial setting of the Psalm. Through-composed settings are almost impossible for effective congregational singing, because congregational singing relies on the use of repeated melodies (as in the repetition of melodies in each stanza of a hymn) or refrains (as in responsorial Psalmody). But they are very effective for soloists or choirs, given their opportunity to rehearse the nuances of more complex music.

Furthermore, several composers — over the span of several centuries — have written compelling musical interpretations of Psalms without text. Emma Lou Diemer and Herbert Howells, for example, have each written several Psalm-based compositions for organ.

To locate solo and choral works based on individual Psalms, consult:

Laster, James. *Catalogue of Choral Music Arranged in Biblical Order*. Second Edition. Lanham: Scarecrow Press, 1996. Volume 1, plus supplement.

———. *Catalogue of Vocal Solos and Duets Arranged in Biblical Order*. Lanham: Scarecrow Press, 1984.

Several publishers also offer on-line scriptural indices for their music.

RECORDINGS

Several choral and vocal solo recordings include Psalm-based selections. For a sampling of recordings devoted exclusively to musical settings of the Psalms, see:

American Psalmody. 3 volumes. Gloria Dei Cantores, Elizabeth C. Patterson, director.

Goostly Psalmes: Anglo-American Psalmody from 1550-1800. Harmonia Mundi, Paul Hillier, conductor, 1996.

Make a Joyful Noise: American Psalmody. Ron Jeffers, conductor. New World Records, 1996.

Psalms. Turtle Creek Chorale, 1999.

Thou Art My Refuge: Psalms of Salvation and Mercy. Gloria Dei Cantores, Elizabeth C. Patterson, director.

The Psalms in Contemporary and Emerging Worship, Psalm-Based Scripture Songs, and the Psalms in Popular Music Idioms

The majority of published resources for using the Psalms in worship were developed for use in what many now think of as "traditional" or "liturgical" worship — though some of them use a folk or jazz musical idiom that is associated with "contemporary" worship. They present a rich repository of pastoral, homiletical, and artistic wisdom, and continue to be used by millions of Christians each week.

Yet many congregations in contemporary or emerging worship traditions may not perceive the potential of this material for their own learning or use. As hundreds of congregations have embraced a variety of newer approaches to worship, many have set aside any Psalm-based music or liturgical texts. When they replaced the organ with the praise team and the hymnal with the media projector, they also set aside the use of the Psalms. Still, the Psalms remain one of the richest sources for inspiration, instruction, and use in worship. In fact, the three largest streams of influence behind various approaches to contemporary or emerging worship each have significant reasons to embrace Psalmody.

- Seeker-sensitive worship, eager to make worship relevant to a particular cultural context for the purpose of evangelism, can find in the Psalter a map of the whole range of human experience. The Psalms can be a powerful way of identifying with the experience of all kinds of people who do not (yet) love God, attend worship, or bother with church.
- Charismatic worship, eager to experience intimacy with God in prayer and worship, can find in the Psalter not only Psalm verses that make good praise choruses but also texts that express lament, penitence, and gratitude.
- Emerging church worship, eager to recover a sense of mystery in worship and personal authenticity and intimacy in community, can hardly find a better source for evocative and challenging images and metaphors.

Many of these possibilities have been recently explored in writings on the Psalms in *Worship Leader* magazine and other recent publications.[66] In contemporary and emerging congregations, the easiest way to incorporate a Psalm might simply be for a worship leader to read the text, perhaps over a simple musical accompaniment by a guitar or band. But once the pastoral and creative possibilities of the Psalter are discovered, there is no end to the creative potential for their use in worship. In fact, each type of Psalmody described in this volume — from choral reading to responsorial Psalmody, met-

66. See articles by Mark Roberts, who is also the author of *No Holds Barred: Wrestling with God in Prayer* (Colorado Springs, CO: Waterbrook Press, 2005), which is closely based on the Psalms. Roberts's work has been commended and cited by a wide range of influential songwriters and contemporary worship leaders, including Matt Redman and Andy Park.

rical Psalmody to chanting — suggests possibilities in contemporary and emerging idioms.

The best place to begin is with the already extant body of Scripture songs based on the Psalms. Over the past thirty years, the biblical Psalms have significantly shaped the development of a variety of contemporary song forms, including the "Praise and Worship" chorus and other worship songs based on various forms of popular music in rock, folk, country, and jazz musical idioms.[67] In fact, the CCLI licensing company has administered the copyright to over 3500 songs based on the Psalms. A significant percentage of these songs are based directly on single verses or memorable images from the Psalms (e.g., "As the Deer," "We Bow Down," and "Shout to the Lord"). These songs have done much to make selected verses of the Psalms well known and well loved.

A desideratum for future composition would be setting larger portions of Psalm texts for reasons described above. The use of Psalm versicles in contemporary Scripture songs finds its closest historical precedent in the versicles used at transition points in the medieval mass. This is not bad in itself, but it does not capture the force and insight of the larger text unless it is complemented by the reading or singing of larger portions of the Psalms. As the surprisingly large size of the following list of recordings suggests, new energy is being given to revitalizing the inclusion of whole Psalm texts in the repertoire of contemporary and emerging worship.

One of the simplest ways to achieve this is to pair short choruses based on a single verse of a Psalm with the reading of the entire Psalm (which results in another type of responsorial Psalmody as described above). For example, Darlene Zschech's "Shout to the Lord" might be paired with a reading of Psalm 65.[68] Or Martin Nystrom's "As the Deer" might be paired with a reading of Psalm 42, the source of its primary imagery. As these songs move from being considered "contemporary" to more traditional, no doubt new compositions will emerge that are also based on verses or images from particular Psalm texts.

67. For more on this theme, see Greg Scheer, "Singing the Psalms in Modern Worship," www.calvin.edu/worship; see also Ron Rienstra, "Singing, Saying, Preaching, Praying: Using the Psalms in Contemporary Worship," *Reformed Worship* 60 (June 2001): 42-43, available at www.reformedworship.org.

68. *Sing! A New Creation* (Grand Rapids: Faith Alive, 2002), hymn #222.

Other contemporary and popular songwriters have begun to write rhapsody-like songs that mirror the structure of specific Psalms or to adapt metrical Psalms into music of a contemporary idiom. The leading example of an individual text is likely U2's setting of Psalm 40, entitled "40" (see the recordings "War" and "Under the Blood Red Sky"). Bono, in fact, is a leading spokesperson for the value of the Psalms in contemporary culture; he has compared the Psalms to blues music.[69]

A number of new recordings in "contemporary" rock or folk-rock style have been produced in the last few years, many by individual congregations or local recording companies:

Barnard, Shane, and Shane Everett. *Psalms.* Franklin, TN: Inpop Records, 2002. www.inpop.com and www.waitingroomministries.com

Becker, Margaret, and David Edwards. *Psalms: Faithfully Yours.* West Monroe, LA: The Select Artist Group/Here To Him Music, 2004.

Brenner, Scott. *King of Glory: Worship from the Book of Psalms.* Franklin, TN: MMV Scott Brenner Music. www.scottbrenner.org

Celtic Psalms: Featuring the Praise and Worship of Eden's Bridge. Brentwood, TN: StraightWay Music (a division of EMI Christian Music Group), 1997.

Field, Paul. *Make a Joyful Noise: Psalms for a New Generation.* Eastbourne: ICC Studios, 2003. www.iccrecords.com (2 CD set).

The Graham Kendrick Psalm Collection. Croydon: Make Way Music, 2002. www.makewaymusic.com

Moss, Brian. *Prayerbook no. 1: New Songs Inspired by the Psalms.* 150 Records, 2005.

Psalms: Series with Kent Henry. 2 volumes. Chesterfield, MO: Kent Henry Ministries, 2000-2001. www.kenthenry.com

Psalms & Hymns: Praying the Bible with Wesley Campbell. Volume 1 produced by Stephen Mullin for YB4 Productions. Kelowna, BC, Canada: Revival Now! Resources Inc. www.revivalnow.com

Sing unto the Lord: The Psalms of David for Daily Living. Brentwood, TN: MMV Martingale Music, LLC. www.martingalemusic.com. Distributed by CBD. A collaboration of twelve songwriters.

Sojourn. *These Things I Remember.* Produced by Mike Cosper; co-produced by

---

69. See Bono, introduction to *The Book of Psalms* (New York: Grove, 1999); see also the discussion in Steve Stockman, *Walk On: The Spiritual Journey of U2,* rev. ed. (Lake Mary, FL: Relevant Books, 2005), pp. 130-32, 169-70.

Eddy Morris. Louisville, KY: The Sojourn Community, 2005. www.sojourn community.com

Sons of Korah. Several recordings that feature Psalm settings. See www.sonsofkor ah.com/discography.

Sword of the Spirit: The Psalm Series. Chesterfield, MO: Kent Henry, 1999. www.kent henrymin.org

Talbot, John Michael. *Songs for Worship,* volumes 1-2. Navarre Corporation, 1992. Several of John Michael Talbot's other recordings also include songs based on the Psalms.

White, Ian. *Psalms.* 6 vols. Little Misty Music. See www.littlemistymusic.com

For reviews of several of these recordings, see Greg Scheer, "Singing the Psalms in Modern Worship," www.calvin.edu/worship.

New publications and recordings in these genres appear almost weekly. Further, several recently published books about worship and worship music by such leading contemporary song writers as Matt Redman and David Crowder are peppered with references to what the Psalms teach about worship.[70]

Basis for Improvised Prayer

The Psalms can also be used well as the basis for newly prepared or extemporaneous prayers.[71] This can happen in any number of ways:

- the use of a Psalm paraphrase that is itself a prayer (see the list of Psalm paraphrases above);
- the adaptation of a Psalm into a prayer;

70. Matt Redman, *The Unquenchable Worshipper* (Ventura, CA: Regal Books, 2001), pp. 27-28; *Blessed Be Your Name: Worshiping God on the Road Marked with Suffering* (Ventura, CA: Regal Books, 2005); *Inside Out Worship: Insights for Passionate and Purposeful Worship* (Ventura, CA: Regal Books, 2005). This last book is full of references to the Psalms, including references to studies of the Psalms by Walter Brueggemann and John Calvin. See also Louie Giglio, *The Air I Breathe: Worship as a Way of Life* (Portland, OR: Multnomah, 2003), p. 50; David A. Crowder, *Praise Habit: Finding God in Sunsets and Sushi* (Colorado Springs, CO: NavPress, 2005), pp. 40-45.

71. For a historical example of this, see Peter Martyr Vermigli, *Sacred Prayers,* trans. and ed. John Patrick Donnelly, S.J. (Kirksville, MO: Sixteenth Century Journal Publishers, 1996).

- the use of a key verse from the Psalm of the week;[72]
- the intentional use of pervasively scriptural language in prayers.[73]

The following example is based on Psalm 121:

No matter where we are, where we are going, or what we are doing,
we know that we find our help in you, our Lord.
You are the creator and sustainer of all
that has been made and will be made.
And yet, the immensity of creation does not distract you
from caring personally for every person in it.
We know that is true of your care for us too!
You do not daydream or become weary in that care.
We thank you that you not only watch over us with diligence
but that you will guide us so that we will not fall —
so that we won't even stumble.
Whether we are awake or asleep, you are there,
sheltering and protecting us from all that would hurt us.
We know that you watch over all our living —
you have in the past, and we know you are now.
Your promise holds for the future and for eternity,
and we praise and thank you for that. Amen.[74]

It is also possible that the structural analysis of a Psalm (see analysis above) might suggest ways of using the Psalms as a guide to structure extemporaneous prayer. Just as the Song of Mary (Luke 1) improvises on the Song of Hannah (1 Samuel 2), so worshipers today can use the Psalms as the basis for improvising our own prayers. Consider using Psalm 51, for example, as the basis for improvising a prayer of confession, as follows:

72. Wallace, *Words to God, Words from God,* p. 128; *The Worship Sourcebook.*
73. H. O. Old models prayers based on Psalms adaptations. See "The Psalms as Prayer," in *Leading in Prayer: A Workbook for Worship* (Grand Rapids: Eerdmans, 1995), and "Praying the Psalms," in *Praying with the Bible* (Louisville: Geneva Press, 1984).
74. *The Worship Sourcebook* (Grand Rapids, MI: Faith Alive/Baker Books, 2004), p. 204 (used by permission). See also Wallace, *Words to God, Words from God,* pp. 120-21.

LEADER 1: Psalm 51:1-6: "Have mercy on me . . ."
LEADER 2: Extemporaneous Prayer of Confession
LEADER 1: Psalm 51:7-12: "Cleanse me . . . create in me a pure heart . . ."
LEADER 2: Extemporaneous Prayer for Renewal
LEADER 1: Psalm 51:13-19: "Then I will teach transgressors your ways . . ."
LEADER 2: Extemporaneous Prayer of Dedication

Or consider taking an entire worship service, perhaps a mid-week prayer service or Thanksgiving Day service, to "pray through" Psalm 33.[75]

RESOURCES FOR ADAPTING THE PSALMS FOR PRAYER

Dunnam, Maxie, and John David Walt, Jr. *Praying the Story: Learning Prayer from the Psalms.* Nashville: Abingdon Press, 2005. See pp. 89-100 for complete prayers based on adaptations of particular Psalms, plus several Psalm excerpts for use during prayer.

Griggs, Donald L. *Praying and Teaching the Psalms.* Nashville: Abingdon, 1984.

Moore, T. M. *The Psalms for Prayer.* Grand Rapids: Baker, 2002. The complete Psalter, with Psalms interspersed with suggested topics for prayers. The introduction also describes several different ways of praying the Psalms: verbatim praying, paraphrase praying, guided praying, and responsive praying. This volume is particularly useful for connecting its materials with other resources in what has broadly been called the "prayer movement" among evangelical Christians.

Patterson, Ward. *Under His Wings: Psalms 1–50* and *Into His Love: Psalms 101–150.* Denver: Accent Books. A series of prayers based on individual Psalms.

Stradling, Leslie E. *Praying the Psalms.* Philadelphia: Fortress Press, 1977. Meditations on over twenty Psalms that prompt ways of praying in light of the text.

Thompson, Marjorie. *Soul Feast: An Invitation to the Christian Spiritual Life.* See pp. 45-46 for suggestions for preparing prayers based on particular Psalms.

75. See, for example, Leroy Christoffels, "In the Pit . . . Waiting: A Service Based on Psalm 40," *Reformed Worship* 34 (Dec. 1994): 9-11. I have also benefited from sample services by Wayne Brouwer, Leroy Christoffels, Norma de Waal Malefyt, and Howard Vanderwell. Several of these are available at www.reformedworship.org (search for "Psalms"), and at www.calvin.edu/worship/psalms. For other examples, see Wild Goose Worship Group, *Sweet Honey and Hard Places: Prayer Services Based on the Psalms* (Glasgow: Iona Community Wild Goose Worship Group, 2005).

In addition to complete Psalm paraphrases, single verses or small portions of a given Psalm can be used as refrains during prayer, such as the familiar refrain from Psalm 136 (and several other Old Testament canticles):

Give thanks to the LORD, for he is good.
God's love endures forever.

Short sections of a Psalm can also be used to begin or end an otherwise extemporaneous prayer, such as:

We pray to you, O LORD;
you hear our voice in the morning;
at sunrise we offer our prayers
and wait for your answer.   (Ps. 5:2-3)

Or,

May the words of our mouths
and the meditations of our hearts
be acceptable in your sight,
O LORD, our Rock and our Redeemer.   (based on Ps. 19:14)

"The Psalms illuminate the mind for the purpose of enkindling the soul, indeed to put it to fire. It may indeed be said that the purpose of the Psalms is to turn the souls into a sort of burning bush."

Stanley Jaki, *Praying the Psalms: A Commentary*

Visual Imagery, Children's Books, Calligraphy

Worship leaders and planners might also look for ways in which visual artists could convey the meaning and significance of particular Psalms. Psalm-based images, whether gleaned from professionally printed materials or commissioned from local artists (or children), could be either projected in some form or printed on worship folders or bulletins. See especially:

Jackson, Donald (artistic director and illuminator). *Psalms*. Collegeville, MN: Liturgical Press, 2006. The second in a seven-volume series of full-color, page-by-page reproductions from the Saint John's Bible.

Kaai, Anneke. *The Psalms: An Artist's Impression*. Downers Grove, IL: InterVarsity Press, 1999. Kaai offers abstract settings of individual Psalms — over twenty four-color renderings.

As with liturgical music, the use of published artwork requires securing copyright permission. Several Psalms are depicted evocatively in books suitable for children (but instructive and inspiring for people of all ages). These books might also suggest new possibilities for children's sermons in places where this is common practice. Reading these books to the children gathered at the front of the sanctuary would engage children with the straightforward words of the biblical text along with their accompanying illustration and would function for others in the congregation as one of the Scripture readings for the day. This practice would minimize the impression that the children's sermon is a time-out from the rest of the liturgy. See the following children's books:

Anderson, Joel. *God Knows Me!* (Psalm 139). Golden Books, 1999.

Bluedorn, Johannah. *Bless the Lord: The 103rd Psalm*, and *The Lord Builds the House: The 127th Psalm*. Trivium Pursuit, 2005.

Chocheli, Niko. *The Praises: Psalm 148*. St. Vladimir's Seminary Press, 2000.

Illustrated Psalms of Praise/Salmos De Alabanza Ilustrados. Illustrated by Amy Ribordy Reese. Chicago: Liturgy Training Publications, 2005.

Ladwig, Tim. *Psalm 23*. Grand Rapids: Eerdmans, 1997.

Le Tord, Bijou. *Sing a New Song: A Book of Psalms*. Grand Rapids: Eerdmans, 1997.

Papademetriou, Dorrie. *Celebrate the Earth: Psalm 104.* St. Vladimir's Seminary Press, 2000.

Webber, Christopher L., and Preston McDaniels (illustrator). *Psalms for Children Series.* Morehouse Publishing. *Shout for Joy and Sing!: Psalm 65 for Children; Praise the Lord, My Soul: Psalm 104 for Children; The Lord Is My Shepherd: Psalm 23 for Children.*

Calligraphy is also a means of rendering the text of the Psalms in memorable, instructive, and inspiring ways. See, for example:

Botts, Timothy. *The Book of Psalms.* Carol Stream, IL: Tyndale House Publishers, 1987.

———. *The Holy Bible, New Living Translation,* Botts illustrated edition. Carol Stream, IL: Tyndale House Publishers, 2000.

Composite Collections of Psalmody

The following volumes include selections of Psalms in multiple styles and formats:

El Himnario. New York: Church Publishing, 1998. A Spanish-language hymnal developed by the Episcopal Church USA, United Church of Christ, and Presbyterian Church USA. See numbers 405-41 for several Spanish-language Psalm settings in both metrical and responsorial formats.

Gather Comprehensive. 2nd edition. Chicago: GIA Publications, 2004.

Journeysongs. 2nd edition. Portland, OR: Oregon Catholic Press.

Leach, Richard, and David Schaap, eds. *The Selah Psalter.* Kingston, NY: Selah Publishing Company, 2001. See also selected examples in David Schaap, ed., *New Songs of Rejoicing.* Selah Publishing, 1994.

Mawby, Colin. *New Psalms for Common Worship.* Kevin Mayhew Publishers.

Perry, Michael, and David Iliff, eds. *Psalms for Today.* London: Hodder & Stoughton, 1990.

Perry, Michael, David Peacock, Christopher Norton, and Chris Rolinson, eds. *Songs from the Psalms.* London: Hodder & Stoughton, 1990.

Psalm Praise. London: Falcon, 1973. Chant and metrical settings for all 150 Psalms.

RitualSong. Chicago: GIA Publications, 1996.

Sing! A New Creation. Grand Rapids: Faith Alive, 2003. Includes over seventy Psalm settings in both metrical and responsorial forms.

Tam, Angela, ed. *Hymns of Universal Praise*. Chinese Christian Literature Council, 2002. Includes thirty Psalms in multiple formats in Chinese and English.

Warren, Norman. *Psalms for the People*. Kevin Mayhew Publishers. Includes settings of over ninety portions of the Psalms found in the lectionary.

Wyatt, Jeff Allan, Paul M. Miller, Lillenas (composite). *The Psalms in Worship: Arrangements from the Psalter for Performance and Liturgy*.

The following recordings including settings of the Psalms in multiple styles and formats:

The Jerusalem Psalter. Hänssler, 2000. Four CDs, with Psalmody from the city of Jerusalem by Catholic, Protestant, and Orthodox congregations.

Psalms for the Soul. The Choir of St. John's, Elora, Ontario, Noel Edison, director. Naxos, 2000.

Refuge and Strength: Selections from the Psalter of the Book of Common Prayer. The choir of the Church of St. Luke in the Fields, conducted by David Shuler. New York: Church Publishing.

Spirituality of the Psalms. The Schola Cantorum of St. Peter the Apostle, J. Michael Thompson, director. Collegeville, MN: Liturgical Press.

Children and Youth in Intergenerational Worship

I must also emphasize that there is nothing about Psalmody that should limit its use to adults. The Psalms offer the kind of honesty and authenticity that adolescent youth long for. They offer to young children a language for worship that is at once vivid, formative, and surprisingly accessible (see the above list of children's books based on the Psalms).

When we think of children and youth praying the Psalms, it immediately suggests the value of appropriate instruction to help them engage the text more meaningfully. It is significant that this instruction is often equally needed by adults! One value of engaging children and youth in praying the Psalms is that it often gently forces congregations to offer better instruction to the whole community.

Several available resources on Psalmody are specifically geared toward children, youth, or intergenerational audiences. See, for example:

Brown, Carolyn C. *Forbid Them Not: Involving Children in Sunday Worship*. 3 volumes. Nashville: Abingdon Press, 1991. Offers suggestions for each Sunday, based on the Revised Common Lectionary, many of which involve the Psalm readings.

Hawn, C. Michael. *Halle, Halle: We Sing the World Round, Songs from the World Church for Children, Youth, and Congregation* (Choristers Guild, 1999), which includes several Psalm refrains that could be used by adult choirs as well as children's choirs.

Witvliet, John D. *A Child Shall Lead: Children in Worship*. Choristers Guild, 1999.

Over 200 anthems for children's and youth choirs based on the Psalms are available from Choristers Guild (see www.choristersguild.org/catalog/).

"The Psalms are inexhaustible, and deserve to be read, said, sung, chanted, whispered, learned by heart, and even shouted from the rooftops. They express all the emotions we are ever likely to feel (including some we hope we may not), and they lay them, raw and open, in the presence of God, like a golden retriever bringing to its master's feet every strange object it finds in the field."

N. T. Wright, *Simply Christian: Why Christianity Makes Sense*

Learning the Psalms by Number

The Psalms can function as meaningful prayer whether or not congregations know they are singing the Psalms and whether or not congregations know what Psalm they are singing or praying. Indeed, these are common occurrences. During the time in which I completed this project, I had the opportunity to visit several very different congregations, each of whom heard readings from the Psalms and sang songs from the Psalms that were in no way identified.

Yet while knowing the Psalm number is not strictly speaking necessary, it is remarkably helpful and wise. There is great value in helping congregations become Psalms-literate by helping them know which Psalms they are using and encouraging them to pray these texts outside of worship.

Biblical literacy comes, in part, by learning to name the parts of the Bible. This is especially noticeable in children. When a child learns to find a text in the Bible, this represents some early knowledge of the Bible and leads to much more efficient future learning. Learning a text by book, chapter, and verse is part of learning the Bible for children of all ages.

To help congregations learn to know the Psalms by number, consider these simple suggestions:

- *If a hymn or song is based on a Psalm, simply list the Psalm number behind it in a printed bulletin or projected order of service: for example, "O Worship the King" (based on Psalm 104).*
- *If spoken prayer will incorporate part of a Psalm, note that in the bulletin: "Our intercessory prayer today will begin with the poignant words of Psalm 63."*
- *Look for a Psalm to recommend to worshipers for their personal prayers, for example: "Continue to meditate on the themes of this week's service by praying Psalm 103," or "In preparation for next week's service, meditate on Psalm 63."*
- *Recommend that worshipers keep a personal Bible and mark the texts from the Psalms (or any part of Scripture) that have been read or sung in worship. There is no reason why young children might not also participate in this practice, learning to build a basic repertoire of favorite Psalms (perhaps beginning with Psalms 23, 100, 139, 150, and then expanding beyond that over time).*

Selecting from among These Methods

The Psalms are enormously varied in style, voice, and tone; it is unfortunate that most congregations and most traditions are familiar with only one form of rendering the Psalms. Ideally, a congregation would have the flexibility to move among various forms — for example, choral reading, metrical Psalmody, and simple chant — in order to choose the form best suited to a particular text. Some texts call for exuberance, others for introspection. Some are conventional; others defy convention. In each congregation, in each cultural context, the musical or dramatic forms that best suit a given Psalm will vary.

It could be that one effect of that flexibility (and of this book) will be to encourage greater experimentation in worship. This is potentially either a very good or very bad thing. Some communities suffer from years of drought when it comes to creativity. Others suffer from endless innovation. Ministry with pastoral poise requires a judicious mix of repetition and innovation, form and freedom, creativity and accountability. While the matter of creativity is the subject for an entire book in itself, let me say briefly that innovation is typically best when it is

- piloted in a small group outside of a congregation's normal worship services (perhaps with a choir or education class — and especially with the children in a congregation);
- explained (best in an educational session, but also through a congregational newsletter or worship bulletin announcement);
- modeled first (perhaps by a soloist or small vocal ensemble), then done with full participation;
- done more than once (it typically takes a while for a new form of participation to become natural); and
- limited to one innovation at a time (it is difficult for most congregations to absorb changes in too many directions at the same time).

Wise, winsome leadership is a key to helping congregations both sense the value of the Psalms and pray them with open hearts and minds.

Finding Sources

The majority of the hymn and Psalm collections mentioned in this survey are available from The Hymn Society in the United States and Canada (1-800-THE-HYMN), from the websites of individual publishers, and through internet websites such as amazon.com. Most Christian resource stores or outlets carry only a small portion of these resources.

Pastoral Postscript

Though the practice of psalmody in worship can be simple and accessible, there is no denying that any call to promoting the Psalms in worship seems daunting. This is particularly true because we live in a period of biblical illiteracy. In such a time, it is tempting to restrict, rather than expand, our use of the Psalter liturgically. As one pastoral leader noted:

> Only in a climate where the Bible is well-known and made a part of the community consciousness can the Psalms be used in a way that allows the faithful to integrate them fully into their spiritual life. For the Psalter is, in a manner, a summary of the Old Testament. It presupposes a knowledge of the law, of the history of Israel, of the prophets and the wisdom literature. Moreover, the Psalter occupies a central place in the understanding of the New Testament and of the person of Jesus and his function in the history of salvation.[1]

Students of the lectionary will sense the same point. Studying the Psalms in the lectionary forces us to ask questions about the meaning of both the Psalm texts before us and the other parts of Scripture to which they lead us.

Yet while the Psalms do require biblical literacy for rich, nuanced use,

---

1. John Eudes Bamberger, foreword to *The Abbey Psalter: The Book of Psalms Used by the Trappist Monks of Genesee Abbey* (New York: Paulist Press, 1981).

they also *promote* biblical literacy. Rather than waiting for biblical literacy to return before resuscitating Psalm singing, it can be pastorally wise to revitalize Psalm singing in local congregations and to undertake whatever education is necessary to make it successful. Patient, winsome promotion of Psalm singing in contextually appropriate ways remains one of the most expedient ways to promote worship that is at once vital and faithful, both relevant and profound.

Another way to explore this theme is to admit frankly that praying the Psalms is difficult, but extremely rewarding. As Dietrich Bonhoeffer testified:

> In many churches the Psalms are read or sung every Sunday, or even daily, in succession. These churches have preserved a priceless treasure, for only with daily use does one appropriate this divine prayer book. When read only occasionally, these prayers are too overwhelming in design and power and tend to turn us back to more palatable fare. But whoever has begun to pray the Psalter seriously and regularly will soon give a vacation to other little devotional prayers and say: "Ah, there is not the juice, the strength, the passion, the fire which I find in the Psalter. It tastes too cold and too hard" (Luther). . . . Whenever the Psalter is abandoned, an incomparable treasure vanishes from the Christian church. With its recovery will come unsuspected power.[2]

Praying the Psalms is not easy, but — like many of life's richest experiences — the practice is well worth the effort. One of the most fruitful ways to approach the challenge of worship leadership is to see it in terms of the rich practice of Christian hospitality.[3] The practice of hospitality is central to the Christian life and the practice of public worship. Among other practices, faithful Christian living is fundamentally about looking for ways to offer the peace

2. Dietrich Bonhoeffer, *Psalms: The Prayer Book of the Bible* (Minneapolis: Augsburg, 1970), pp. 25-26.

3. For more on this theme, see Reinhard Hütter, "Hospitality and Truth: The Disclosure of Practices in Worship and Doctrine," in *Practicing Theology: Beliefs and Practices in the Christian Life,* ed. Miroslav Volf and Dorothy C. Bass (Grand Rapids: Eerdmans, 2002), pp. 220-22; Christine Pohl, *Making Room: Recovering Hospitality as a Christian Tradition* (Grand Rapids: Eerdmans, 1999), pp. 182-83; John Ferguson, "Hospitable Leadership of Songs for Worship," in *Discerning the Spirits: A Guide to Thinking about Christian Worship Today,* ed. Cornelius Plantinga Jr. and Sue A. Rozeboom (Grand Rapids: Eerdmans, 2003), pp. 117-19.

"Words and music did for me what solid, even rigorous, religious argument could never do, they introduced me to God, not belief in God, more an experiential sense of God. Over art, literature, reason, the way in to my spirit was a combination of words and music. As a result, the book of Psalms always felt open to me. . . ."

Bono, Introduction to *The Book of Psalms*

of Christ to all fellow pilgrims, to embrace the stranger and the orphan, to minister to the deepest needs of each other's souls. Faithful Christian worship is, at its core, a place where the practice of hospitality should flourish. This practice is first of all God's practice, as God welcomes us to the waters of baptism, the feast of the Lord's Supper, the nourishment of the Word, and the encouragement of the assembly. And then hospitality becomes our practice, as we greet each other in Jesus' name, pray for each other, respond together to the Word, and extend the feasting of the table into lives of joyful and obedient Christian service.

Hospitality is a practice that involves profound sensitivity to the needs of the guest, the seeker, the weak, and the strong. However, the best hospitality practices attention beyond our *felt* needs to our *ultimate* needs. The exemplary host offers both water and living Water, both a warm welcome and practices that will sustain us in difficult days. And that is where the Psalms are especially crucial. The Psalms address fundamental human needs. They give voice to the whole range of human experience. They invite us in to the shared experience of believers in every time and place. The Psalms themselves are an invitation to a spiritual feast.

An ancient fourth-century church order, the *Apostolic Constitutions*, gives good instructions for all leaders of public worship: "Be a builder up, a converter, apt to teach, forbearing of evil, of a gentle mind, meek, long-suffering, ready to exhort, ready to comfort, as one of God." Only then does this ancient church order go on to speak of skill: "When you call together an assembly of the Church, it is as if you were the commander of a great ship. Set up the enterprise to be accomplished with all possible skill, charging the deacons as mariners to prepare places for the congregation as for passengers, with all due care and decency."[4]

These instructions point to hospitality as one of the key virtues of a thoughtful worship leader. Serving as a worship leader is like serving as a host for a voyage or a feast. The goal is to guide worshipers through the feast of worship: to help them feed on God's Word, to help them feel connected as a community, to help them participate fully in every aspect of the service — all for the glory of God. We need our most disciplined, creative, and earnest poets, pastors, preachers, educators, musicians, and artists to take up their priestly roles in the Christian community and bring the Psalms to life in ways that form us for faithful and obedient service.

May God's Spirit strengthen all of us who lead God's people, and help us all to grow in grace and in our desire to worship the Lord in spirit and truth.

4. *Ante-Nicene Fathers,* vol. VII (Grand Rapids: Eerdmans, 1979), p. 421.

Modern Testimonies

Dorothy Day (1897-1980) The Psalms became part of my child-
hood. There was a small Episcopal
church on Thirty-fifth Street and Cottage Grove Avenue. Dr. Wilson,
the rector, called on my father when he was writing his book. Father
was embarrassed because of the highball and plate of cigarette stubs by
his side. Dr. Wilson was making a door-to-door visit in his parish, and
when he heard my mother had been brought up in the Episcopal
Church, he persuaded her to send the boys to sing in the choir and play
in the gymnasium. I went to church too every Sunday and admired my
brothers in their cassocks and surplices, and was much attracted to a
blond boy soprano soloist named Russell. I loved the Psalms and the
Collect prayers and learned many of them by heart, and the anthems
filled me with joy. . . .

Whenever I felt the beauty of the world in song or story, in the material universe around me, or glimpsed it in human love, I wanted to cry
out with joy. The Psalms were an outlet for this enthusiasm of joy or grief
— and I suppose my writing was also an outlet. After all, one must communicate ideas. I always felt the common unity of our humanity; the
longing of the human heart is for this communion. If only I could sing, I
thought, I would shout before the Lord, and call upon the world to shout
with me, "All ye works of the Lord, bless ye the Lord, praise Him and glo-
rify Him forever." My idea of heaven became one of fields and meadows,

sweet with flowers and songs and melodies unutterable, in which even the laughing gull and the waves on the shore would play their part.

Dorothy Day, *The Long Loneliness* (San Francisco: Harper & Row, Publishers, 1952)

Thomas Merton (1915-1968)

It is supremely important for those who read the Psalms and chant them in the public prayer of the Church to grasp, if they can, the poetic content of these great songs. The poetic gift is not one that has been bestowed on all men with equal lavishness and that gift is unfortunately necessary not only for the writers of poems but also, to some extent, for those who read them. This does not mean that the recitation of the Divine Office is an aesthetic recreation whose full possibilities can only be realized by initiates endowed with refined taste and embellished by a certain artistic cultivation. But it does mean that the type of reader whose poetic appetites are fully satisfied by the Burma Shave rhymes along our American highways may find it rather hard to get anything out of the Psalms. I believe, however, that the reason why so many fail to understand the Psalms — beyond the fact that they are never quite at home even with Church Latin — is that latent poetic faculties have never been awakened in their spirits by someone capable of pointing out to them that the Psalms really are poems.

Thomas Merton, *Bread in the Wilderness* (New York: New Directions Publishing Corporation, 1953), p. 53

There is no aspect of the interior life, no kind of religious experience, no spiritual need of man that is not depicted and lived out in the

Psalms. But we cannot lay hands on these riches unless we are willing to work for them. The work to be done has been suggested above. It is no longer so much a matter of study, since the study has been done for us by experts. We need only to take advantage of the texts they have given us, and use them with faith, and confidence and love. Above all we need zeal and strength and perseverance. We cannot by mere human ingenuity or talent exhaust all that is contained in the Psalms. Indeed, if we seek only to "get something out of them" we will perhaps get less than we expect, and generous efforts may be frustrated because they are turned in the wrong direction: toward ourselves rather than toward God.

In the last analysis, it is not so much what we get out of the Psalms that rewards us, as what we put into them. If we really make them our prayer, really prefer them to other methods and expedients, in order to let God pray in us in His own words, and if we sincerely desire above all to offer Him this particularly pure homage of our Christian faith, then indeed we will enter into the meaning of the Psalms, and they will become our favorite vocal prayers.

Thomas Merton, *Praying the Psalms* (Collegeville, MN: The Liturgical Press, 1956), pp. 44-45

The spiritual understanding of the Psalter will therefore not introduce us to some esoteric technique of prayer, nor will it tempt us to induce within our minds some peculiar psychological state. It will, above all, tell us not merely what we ought to be but the unbelievable thing that we already *are*. It will tell us over and over again that we are Christ in this world, and that He lives in us, and that what was said of Him has been and is being fulfilled in us: and that the last, most perfect fulfillment of all is now, at this moment, by the theological virtue of hope, placed in our hands. Thus the liturgy of earth is necessarily one with the liturgy of heaven. We are at the same time in the desert and in the Promised Land. The Psalms are our Bread of Heaven in the wilderness of our Exodus.

Thomas Merton, *Bread in the Wilderness* (New York: New Directions Publishing Corporation, 1953), p. 38

Dietrich Bonhoeffer (1906-1945)   Now there is in the Holy Scriptures a book which is distinguished from all other books of the Bible by the fact that it contains only prayers. The book is the Psalms. It is at first very surprising that there is a prayerbook in the Bible. The Holy Scripture is the Word of God to us. But prayers are the words of men. How do prayers then get into the Bible? Let us make no mistake about it, the Bible is the Word of God even in the Psalms. Then are these prayers to God also God's own word? That seems rather difficult to understand. We grasp it only when we remember that we can learn true prayer only from Jesus Christ, from the word of the Son of God, who lives with us men, to God the Father, who lives in eternity. Jesus Christ has brought every need, every joy, every gratitude, every hope of men before God. In his mouth the word of man becomes the Word of God, and if we pray his prayer with him, the Word of God becomes once again the word of man. All prayers of the Bible are such prayers which we pray together with Jesus Christ, in which he accompanies us, and through which he brings us into the presence of God. Otherwise there are no true prayers, for only in and with Jesus Christ can we truly pray.

If we want to read and to pray the prayers of the Bible and especially the Psalms, therefore, we must not ask first what they have to do with us, but what they have to do with Jesus Christ. We must ask how we can understand the Psalms as God's Word, and then we shall be able to pray them. It does not depend, therefore, on whether the Psalms express adequately that which we feel at a given moment in our heart. If we are to pray aright, perhaps it is quite necessary that we pray contrary to our own heart. Not what we want to pray is important, but what God wants us to pray. If we were dependent entirely on ourselves, we would probably pray only the fourth petition of the Lord's Prayer. But God wants it otherwise. The richness of the Word of God ought to determine our prayer, not the poverty of our heart.

Thus if the Bible also contains a prayerbook, we learn from this that not only that Word which he has to say to us belongs to the Word of God, but also that word which he wants to hear from us, because it is the word of his beloved Son. This is pure grace, that God tells us how we can speak with him and have fellowship with him. We can do it by praying in the name of Jesus Christ. The Psalms are given to us to this end, that we may learn to pray them in the name of Jesus Christ.

In response to the request of the disciples, Jesus gave them the Lord's Prayer. Every prayer is contained in it. Whatever is included in the petitions of the Lord's Prayer is prayed aright; whatever is not included is no prayer. All the prayers of Holy Scripture are summarized in the Lord's Prayer, and are contained in its immeasurable breadth. They are not made superfluous by the Lord's Prayer but constitute the inexhaustible richness of the Lord's Prayer as the Lord's Prayer is their summation. Luther says of the Psalter: "It penetrates the Lord's Prayer and the Lord's Prayer penetrates it, so that it is possible to understand one on the basis of the other and to bring them into joyful harmony." Thus the Lord's Prayer becomes the touchstone for whether we pray in the name of Jesus Christ or in our own name. It makes good sense, then, that the Psalter is often bound together in a single volume with the New Testament. It is the prayer of the Christian church. It belongs to the Lord's Prayer.

Dietrich Bonhoeffer, *Psalms: Prayerbook of the Bible* (Minneapolis: Augsburg Publishing House, 1970), pp. 13-16

Eugene Peterson (b. 1932)   When we go to prayer in the Psalms we find, often to our surprise, that we have been ushered to a pew in the vigorously rich worship of Israel. When David organized Israel into a worshiping congregation, thirty-eight thousand Levites were assigned to provide the leadership and support required (1 Chron. 23:3). Prayer in Israel was not left up to individuals to do or not do as they more or less felt inclined. This was a public works project of impressive dimensions. It was neither private nor peripheral. Common worship takes precedence over private devotions.

Selah, scattered randomly through the Psalms seventy-one times, is the evidence. The word never occurs within the text itself but alongside as a notation in the margin. No one is sure of its exact meaning; scholars guess "pause for a benediction" perhaps, or "louder here — *fortissimo!*" What is beyond guesswork is that it is telltale evidence of liturgy. Like detectives sifting through clues we find *Selah;* from it we deduce not a crime but a community. People were gathered together in prayer by and in these psalms. Congregations were assembled in worship. These prayers are not from the pen of solitary mystics; these are the trained voices of choirs lifting their voices in lament and praise, in petition and adoration.

These psalms that teach us to pray are, all of them, prayers of people gathered as a community before God in worship. Some of them most certainly originated in solitude, and all of them have been continued in solitude. But in the form in which they come to us, the *only* form in which they come to us, and therefore in the way they serve as our school of prayer, they are the prayers of the community before God in worship. Prayer is fundamentally liturgical. *Selah,* untranslated and untranslatable, strewn through the Psalms, will not let us forget it. If its *meaning* is an enigma, its use is clear: *Selah* directed people who were *together* in prayer to do something or other *together.* Our prayer book, by the time we get our hands on it, has all these liturgical scribbles in the margins. Biblically, we are not provided with a single prayer for private devotions. The community in prayer, not the individual at prayer, is basic and primary. The Americanization of prayer has reversed this clear biblical (and human!) order. Individuals don't "make up" the community; they are produced by it. The Psalms return us to this beginning, this original matrix of humanity and spirituality.

Prayer requires community. Prayer is not possible outside of, apart from, or in spite of the praying community. God calls to his people to come before him and hear his word, to obey his commands and receive his blessings. We hear the call and come. We bow our heads and close our eyes. We pray. We open our eyes, look around and see, sometimes to our great surprise, that others are there also. Helmer Ringgren told us bluntly: "The Psalms were not written for private use." We were not invited, it seems, to a private audience with our God.

The assumption that prayer is what we do when we are alone — the solitary soul before God — is an egregious, and distressingly persistent, error. We imagine a lonely shepherd on the hills composing lyrics to the glory of God. We imagine a beleaguered soul sinking in a swamp of trouble calling for help. But our imaginations betray us. We are part of something before we are anything, and never more so than when we pray. Prayer begins in community.

Eugene Peterson, *Answering God: The Psalms as Tools for Prayer* (San Francisco: Harper and Row, 1989), pp. 83-84

A Brief Set of Exercises for Classroom Use

This book is appropriate for use in classes in Old Testament, preaching, worship, and church music. Teachers might consider adapting some of the following exercises for classroom use.

1. Find two or three musical settings of a particular Psalm. Compare how faithful they are to the biblical text, and how well they encourage the congregation to participate in the unique dimensions of the text.

2. Imagine preaching on a particular Psalm. Explain how you would want the Psalm rendered in worship in a different way after your sermon than before it. List the different ways that the Psalm or portion of the Psalm could be incorporated throughout a given worship service or liturgy.

3. Prepare a text for a prayer that is based on a free paraphrase or adaptation of a given Psalm.

4. Prepare a paper on one of the themes in the first part of this volume, explaining how some specific Psalms might be rendered in worship in ways that make these themes clear.

5. Identify a group of two or three Psalms that would be especially appropriate for use in both worship and in pastoral care visits in hospitals, nursing homes, or prisons. Prepare a brief introductory statement for how you would introduce those Psalms in both a worship and pastoral care setting.

6. Prepare a one-sentence introduction to a Psalm text that could be spoken

in worship (or a three-sentence introduction that could be printed in an order of service) to help worshipers pray it more knowingly.

7. Prepare a reader's commentary on a given Psalm, suggesting how a public reading can best interpret the text. Footnote your gleanings from commentaries, looking for ways in which an academic study of the text could be reflected in oral interpretation.

8. With an interlinear translation and academic commentary of the Hebrew text at your side, compare at least four translations or paraphrases of a given Psalm. List improvisations on the text that you find both textually faithful and lyrically compelling. Also list improvisations that you find to be unfaithful to the text or lyrically ponderous.

9. Take a particular Psalm, imagine a non-church-going friend or acquaintance, and write a brief letter to that person explaining how that Psalm might speak to his or her life.

APPENDIX 2

Some Creative Thinking about Worship Renewal

In our work at the Calvin Institute of Christian Worship, we have been privileged for the last seven years to administer a Worship Renewal Grants Program, which has awarded over 300 grants to congregations in a wide variety of denominations. As grant recipients prepare their proposals, we invite them to consider the following statement:

> Worship renewal cannot be reduced to a formula or generated by a set of techniques. We invite you to prayerful consideration of the dynamics or hallmarks of worship renewal, which we continue to learn about from congregations.

- Worship renewal is not something that human ingenuity or creativity can produce or engineer, but is a gift of God's Spirit. Renewal is a gift for which we pray, not an accomplishment we achieve.
- Worship renewal mines the riches of Scripture and leads worshipers to deeper encounters with the message of the gospel.
- Worship renewal arises out of and leads to the full, conscious, and active participation of all worshipers — young and old, the powerless and powerful, newcomers and lifelong worshipers.
- Worship renewal leads a congregation beyond itself, to give itself in ministry to the needs of the local community and the world.
- Worship renewal happens best in healthy congregations, which are

marked by honesty, integrity, unity, and pastoral concern for each worshiper.

Pastoral worship leaders who yearn for renewal begin by asking thoughtful questions about the purpose and meaning of worship before addressing the style or mechanics of worship. A worship committee, a board, pastoral staff, or worship team might begin by asking questions such as:

- How can we help our congregation pray more honestly and deeply through the words we speak and the music we sing together?
- How can we proclaim the gospel message more meaningfully through proclamation, music, and the arts?
- How can we practice Christian hospitality in worship more intentionally?
- How can we celebrate baptism and the Lord's Supper in more profound and significant ways?
- What practices will form our congregation more richly in the contours of the Christian faith?
- How can we improve patterns of communication among worship leaders and between our leaders and all members of the congregation?

These questions will eventually lead to suggestions regarding worship practices and style, but they begin by probing deeper issues about worship.

A COLLABORATIVE EFFORT to lead a community in praying the Psalms more intentionally would speak to nearly every one of these basic questions. In working through this volume, it occurred to me that the Institute, over the past seven years, has not yet received one proposal (from among over 1,500 submitted) that approached worship renewal by attempting to promote praying the Psalms. But what a good idea that could be — with or without grant funding!

Suppose, for example, that a congregation's leadership:

- chose a balanced diet of fifteen (or thirty) Psalms;
- looked for contextually appropriate musical settings for each;

- agreed to use one Psalm in worship each week for 6 months or a year;
- featured the Psalms in sermons and educational settings, with people of all ages;
- provided resources for praying those Psalms in personal and family settings;
- prayed those Psalms in pastoral care settings;
- created resources for spiritual seekers that could demonstrate the power of these texts to speak to their situation in life; and
- engaged local artists, dramatists, and songwriters in preparing creative and thoughtful ways of engaging these texts.

An approach to praying the Psalms need not be complicated or inaccessible. It simply needs to be intentional and pastoral.

Worship renewal is often approached in North American congregations by the development of elaborate programming. We add new worship services, purchase new equipment, and look for more engaging modes of preaching, technology, or singing. These efforts have their place. Yet, if history has anything to teach us, it could be much more fruitful to put our energies into forming congregations through some of the most robust scriptural resources available to us.

General Bibliography

Extensive bibliographies have already been suggested in the footnotes and in the resource sections of this paper. The following is a supplemental list of significant general sources in the history, theology, and practice of the Psalms.

For musical and dramatic settings of the Psalms, recommended recordings, preaching resources, classroom exercises, and updated information about new Psalms publications, visit the Calvin Institute of Christian Worship at www.calvin.edu/worship/psalms. Publishers, composers, artists, preachers, and worship planners who wish to have their resources listed are invited to submit Psalm-related materials to: Psalm Resources, Calvin Institute of Christian Worship, 1855 Knollcrest Circle SE, Grand Rapids, MI 49546-4402.

I. THE PSALMS IN WORSHIP

A. The History of Psalms in Worship

There are several hundred available volumes that probe the history of the Psalms in worship. These resources are among the most available sources, and their bibliographies will provide easy access to the vast majority of significant resources.

HISTORICAL OVERVIEWS

Attridge, Harold W., and Margot E. Fassler. *Psalms in Community: Jewish and Christian Textual, Liturgical and Artistic Traditions.* Atlanta: Society of Biblical Literature, 2003.

Holladay, William. *The Psalms Through Three Thousand Years.* Minneapolis: Fortress Press, 1993.

Lamb, J. A. *The Psalms in Christian Worship.* London: Faith Press, 1962.

Old, Hughes Oliphant. *The Reading and Preaching of the Scriptures in the Worship of the Christian Church.* 5 volumes to date. Grand Rapids: Eerdmans, 1997- . Following the "Psalms" entries in Old's indices offers a close-up view of specific ways the Psalms have been preached in the history of worship.

Shepherd, Massey H., Jr. *The Psalms in Christian Worship: A Practical Guide.* Minneapolis: Augsburg Publishing House, 1976.

Westermeyer, Paul. *Te Deum: The Church and Music.* Minneapolis: Fortress Press, 1998. See the index for references to Psalms and Psalters.

See also, more generally, *Cambridge History of the Bible.* 3 volumes. Cambridge: Cambridge University Press, 1963, 1969, 1970.

EARLY AND MEDIEVAL CHURCH

Fischer, Balthasar. *Die Psalmen als Stimme der Kirche: gesammelte Studien zur christlichen Psalmenfrommigkeit.* Trier: Paulinus-Verlag, 1982.

Heffernan, Thomas J., and E. Ann Matter. *The Liturgy of the Medieval Church.* Kalamazoo: Medieval Institute Publications, 2001.

Hiley, David. *Western Plainchant: A Handbook.* Oxford: Clarendon, 1993.

McKinnon, James. *Music in Early Christian Literature.* Cambridge: Cambridge University Press, 1987. See the extensive list of references for Psalmody in the index.

Stapert, Calvin R. "Singing Psalms from Bible Times to the Protestant Reformation." In *Psalter Hymnal Handbook,* ed. Emily R. Brink and Bert Polman. Grand Rapids: CRC Publications, 1998.

———. *A New Song for an Old World.* Grand Rapids: Eerdmans, 2007. A volume on musical thought in the early church; see especially chapter 10.

Brink, Emily R. "Metrical Psalmody: A Tale of Two Traditions." *Reformed Liturgy and Music* 23 (Winter 1989): 3-8.

Brink, Emily R., and John D. Witvliet. "Contemporary Developments in Music in Reformed Churches Worldwide." In *Christian Worship in Reformed Churches Past and Present*, ed. Lukas Vischer, pp. 324-47. Grand Rapids: Eerdmans, 2003.

Davies, Horton. *The Worship of the American Puritans*. Morgan, PA: Soli Deo Gloria Publications, 1999. See especially chapter 5.

————. *The Worship of the English Puritans*. Morgan, PA: Soli Deo Gloria Publications, 1997. See especially chapter 10.

Leaver, Robin A. *'Goostly Psalmes and Spirituall Songes': English and Dutch Metrical Psalms from Coverdale to Utenhove, 1535-1566*. Oxford: Clarendon Press, 1991. The most comprehensive scholarly study of metrical Psalmody in the sixteenth century.

Patrick, Millar. *Four Centuries of Scottish Psalmody*. London: Oxford University Press, 1949.

Stackhouse, Rochele. *The Language of the Psalms in Worship*. Lanham, MD: Scarecrow Press, 1997.

Temperley, Nicholas. *The Music of the English Parish Church*. 2 volumes. Cambridge: Cambridge University Press, 1979, 2005.

Wilson, Ruth M. *Anglican Chant and Chanting in England, Scotland, and America, 1660 to 1820*. Oxford: Oxford University Press, 1997.

B. Theological, Literary, and Devotional Guides to the Psalms in Worship

Of the many volumes that introduce the Psalms in general, the following pay particular attention to the role and function of the Psalms in worship.

Brueggemann, Walter. *Praying the Psalms*. Winona, MN: Saint Mary's Press, 1982.

————. *The Psalms and the Life of Faith*. Minneapolis: Fortress Press, 1995.

Costen, Melva Wilson. "Liturgy: Praising God." In *Ordo: Bath, Word, Prayer, Table*, ed. Dirk G. Lange and Dwight W. Vogel. Akron: OSL Publications, 2005.

Human, Dirk J., and Cas J. A. Vos, eds. *Psalms and Liturgy*. London: T&T Clark, 2004.

Jinkins, Michael. *In the House of the Lord: Inhabiting the Psalms of Lament.* Collegeville, MN: Liturgical Press, 1998.

Kidd, Reggie M. *With One Voice: Discovering Christ's Song in Our Worship.* Grand Rapids: Baker Books, 2005. See especially chapters 2-4.

Leijssen, L., ed. *Les Psaumes: prières de l'humanité, d'Israël, de l'Église: hommage à Jos Luyten [The Psalms: prayers of humanity, prayers of Israel, prayers of the Church: a tribute to Jos Luyten].* Leuven: Abdij Keizerberg, 1990.

Merton, Thomas. *Bread in the Wilderness.* New York: New Directions, 1953.

Peterson, Eugene. *Answering God: The Psalms as Tools for Prayer.* San Francisco: Harper and Row, 1989.

————. *A Long Obedience in the Same Direction: Discipleship in an Instant Society.* Downers Grove, IL: InterVarsity Press, 2000.

Stuhlmueller, Carroll. *The Spirituality of the Psalms.* Collegeville, MN: Liturgical Press, 2002.

Vos, Cas J. A. "Psalms in Liturgy." In *The Poetry of the Psalms.* London: T&T Clark, 2005.

Wallace, Howard Neil. *Words to God, Word from God: The Psalms in the Prayer and Preaching of the Church.* Burlington, VT: Ashgate, 2005.

Ward, Rowland S. *The Psalms in Christian Worship: A Doctrinal, Historical, and Expository Guide.* Melbourne: Presbyterian Church of Eastern Australia, 1992.

C. Resources on the Practice of Psalmody in Worship

The following books and articles are concerned primarily with how to render the Psalms in worship.

Bourgeault, Cynthia. *Chanting the Psalms: A Practical Guide with Instructional CD.* New Seeds, 2006.

————. *Singing the Psalms: How to Chant in the Christian Contemplative Tradition.* Sounds True, 1998.

Box, Reginald, SSF. *Make Music to Our God: How We Sing the Psalms in Worship.* London: SPCK, 1996.

Coddaire, Louis, and Louis Weil. "The Use of the Psalter in Worship." *Worship* 52 (1978): 342-48.

Duba, Arlo. "Liberating the Psalter." *Reformed Liturgy and Music* 14, no. 4 (1980): 27.

Eaton, J. H. *The Psalms Come Alive: An Introduction to the Psalms Through the Arts.* London: Mowbray, 1984.

Frost, David L. *Making the Liturgical Psalter.* Bramcote, UK: Grove Books, 1981.

Hostetter, B. David. *Psalms and Prayers for Congregational Participation.* Lima, OH: C.S.S. Publishing Co., 1982.

The Hymn 33, no. 2 (April 1982). Theme issue on Psalmody, with articles by Paul Westermeyer, Virginia Folkerts, Carl Schalk, Oliver C. Rupprecht, Mark Bangert, and Leslie Brandt.

Johnson, Terry L. "Restoring Psalm Singing to Our Worship." In *Give Praise to God: A Vision for Reforming Worship,* ed. Philip Graham Ryken, Derek W. H. Thomas, and L. Ligon Duncan III, pp. 257-86. Phillipsburg, NJ: Presbyterian and Reformed Publishing, 2003.

Lamb, J. A. *The Psalms in Christian Worship.* London: Faith Press, 1962.

—————. "The Liturgical Use of the Psalter." *Studia Liturgica* 3 (1964): 65-77.

Leaver, Robin, David Mann, and David Parkes. *Ways of Singing the Psalms.* Collins Liturgical Publications, 1984.

Old, Hughes Oliphant. "Praying the Psalms." In *Praying with the Bible.* Louisville: Geneva Press, 1984.

—————. "The Psalms as Prayer." In *Leading in Prayer: A Workbook for Worship.* Grand Rapids: Eerdmans, 1995.

—————. *Worship: Reformed according to Scripture.* Louisville: Westminster John Knox Press, 2002. See several references to the Psalms in the index.

Pilot Study on a Liturgical Psalter. International Commission on English in the Liturgy. Washington, DC, 1982.

Polman, Bert. "Singing the Psalms Anew." In *Sing! A New Creation.* Leader's Edition. Grand Rapids: Faith Alive, 2002.

The Psalter: Psalms and Canticles for Singing. Louisville: Westminster John Knox Press, 1993. See the introduction.

Reformed Liturgy and Music 23, no. 1 (1989). Theme issue on Psalmody.

Reid, Stephen Breck. *Psalms and Practice: Worship, Virtue, and Authority.* Collegeville, MN: Liturgical Press, 2001. See especially part II for seven volumes on the function of the Psalms in worship.

Routley, Erik. "The Psalms in Today's Church." *Reformed Liturgy and Music* 14 (1980): 20-26.

—————. *Musical Leadership in the Church.* Nashville: Abingdon Press, 1967. See especially pp. 67-86.

Shepherd, Massey H., Jr. *The Psalms in Christian Worship: A Practical Guide.* Minneapolis: Augsburg Publishing House, 1976.

"Singing the Psalms and Canticles in Corporate Worship." In *The New Century Psalter.* Cleveland: Pilgrim Press, 1999.

Williams, Kenneth E. "Ways to Sing the Psalms." *Reformed Liturgy and Music* 18, no. 1 (1984): 12-16.

Witvliet, John D. "Lament." In *Worship Seeking Understanding.* Grand Rapids: Baker Academic, 2003.

D. The Psalms in Eastern Orthodoxy and Eastern and Western Monasticism

These volumes offer access to the rich tradition of worship and use of the Psalms in both Eastern Orthodoxy and Western monasticism (Note: these are two distinct topics, but the literature about them often analyzes them together).

Bradshaw, Paul F. *Two Ways of Praying.* Nashville: Abingdon Press, 1995.

Dyer, Joseph. "The Psalms in Monastic Prayer." In *The Place of the Psalms in the Intellectual Culture of the Middle Ages,* ed. Nancy Van Deusen. Albany, NY: State University of New York Press, 1999.

Fassler, Margot E., and Rebecca A. Baltzer. *The Divine Office in the Middle Ages: Methodology and Source Studies, Regional Developments, Hagiography.* Oxford: Oxford University Press, 2000.

Guiver, George. *Company of Voices: Daily Prayer and the People of God.* New York: Pueblo Publishing Company, 1988.

Lingas, Alexander. "Tradition and Renewal in Contemporary Greek Orthodox Psalmody." In *Psalms in Community: Jewish and Christian Textual, Liturgical, and Artistic Traditions,* ed. Harold W. Attridge and Margot E. Fassler. Atlanta: Society of Biblical Literature, 2003.

Manley, Johanna. *Grace for Grace: The Psalter and the Holy Fathers.* Menlo Park, CA: Monastery Books, 1992. See p. 703 for a liturgical concordance regarding the use of the Psalms in Orthodox, Catholic, and Episcopalian liturgies.

McKinnon, James W. "The Book of Psalms, Monasticism, and the Western Liturgy." In *The Place of the Psalms in the Intellectual Culture of the Middle Ages,* ed. Nancy Van Deusen. Albany, NY: State University of New York Press, 1999.

Reardon, Patrick Henry. *Christ in the Psalms.* Ben Lomond, CA: Conciliar Press, 2000.

Rouguet, A. M. *The Liturgy of the Hours.* Collegeville, MN: Liturgical Press, 1971.

Taft, Robert. "Christian Liturgical Psalmody: Origins, Development, Decomposition, Collapse." In *Psalms in Community: Jewish and Christian Textual, Liturgical, and Artistic Traditions,* ed. Harold W. Attridge and Margot E. Fassler. Atlanta: Society of Biblical Literature, 2003.

———. *The Liturgy of the Hours in East and West: The Origins of the Hours in East and West.* Collegeville, MN: The Liturgical Press, 1986.

Uspensky, Nicholas. *Evening Worship in the Orthodox Church.* Ed. and trans. Paul Lazor. Crestwood, NY: St. Vladimir's Seminary Press, 1985.

Woolfenden, Gregory W. *Daily Liturgical Prayer: Origins and Theology.* Burlington, VT: Ashgate, 2004.

E. The Case for Exclusive Psalmody

Some denominations and congregations in the Reformed and Presbyterian traditions have maintained the practice of Calvin's Geneva, Scottish Presbyterianism, and the English and New England Puritans of singing exclusively from the Psalms. A significant number of volumes have been produced throughout the last four centuries to defend this practice. The following books offer an entry point into this literature; see their bibliographies for additional sources.

Bushell, Michael. *The Songs of Zion: A Contemporary Case for Exclusive Psalmody.* Crown and Covenant Publications, 1993.

McNaughter, John. *The Psalms in Worship.* Pittsburgh: United Presbyterian Board of Publications, 1902, 1992. Available from Still Waters Publications.

Stewart, Bruce C. *Psalm Singing Revisited: The Case for Exclusive Psalmody.* Crown and Covenant Publications, 1999.

Williamson, G. I. *The Singing of Psalms in the Worship of God.* Phillipsburg, NJ: Presbyterian and Reformed Publishing.

II. General Bibliography on the Psalms

A. Introductions to the Psalms

These volumes provide an overall orientation to the Psalms, analyze challenges in interpreting the texts, and describe various types of Psalms. These volumes typically assume no scholarly background in Psalms studies, but they do introduce readers to the scholarly literature and themes.

Anderson, Bernard. *Out of the Depths.* 3rd ed. Louisville: Westminster John Knox Press, 2000.

Bellinger, W. H., Jr. *Psalms: Reading and Studying the Book of Praises.* Peabody, MA: Hendrickson, 1990.

Crenshaw, James. *The Psalms: An Introduction.* Grand Rapids: Eerdmans, 2001.

DeClaissé-Walford, Nancy L. *Introduction to the Psalms: A Song from Ancient Israel.* St. Louis: Chalice Press, 2004.

Hopkins, Denise Dombrowski. *Journey through the Psalms.* St. Louis: Chalice Press, 2002.

Interpretation: A Journal of Bible and Theology (April 1992). Theme issue on the Psalms.

Longman, Tremper, III. *How to Read the Psalms.* Downers Grove, IL: InterVarsity Press, 1999.

Mays, James Luther. *The Lord Reigns: A Theological Handbook to the Psalms.* Louisville: Westminster John Knox Press, 1994.

McCann, J. Clinton, Jr. *A Theological Introduction to the Book of Psalms: The Psalms as Torah.* Nashville: Abingdon Press, 1993.

Miller, Patrick D., Jr. *Interpreting the Psalms.* Philadelphia: Fortress Press, 1986.

Murphy, Roland E. *The Psalms Are Yours.* Mahwah, NJ: Paulist Press, 1993.

Pleins, J. David. *The Psalms: Songs of Tragedy, Hope, and Justice.* Maryknoll, NY: Orbis Books, 1993.

Reid, Stephen Breck. *Listening In: A Multicultural Reading of the Psalms.* Nashville: Abingdon Press, 1997.

Seybold, Klaus. *Introducing the Psalms.* Edinburgh: T&T Clark, 1990.

B. Commentaries on the Psalms

These volumes provide commentary on individual Psalm texts.

Brueggemann, Walter. *The Message of the Psalms: A Theological Commentary.* Minneapolis: Augsburg Publishing, 1984.

Davidson, Robert. *The Vitality of Worship: A Commentary on the Book of Psalms.* Grand Rapids: Eerdmans, 1998.

Jaki, Stanley L. *Praying the Psalms: A Commentary.* Grand Rapids: Eerdmans, 2001. Brief, prayer-oriented comments on each Psalm.

Kraus, H. J. *Psalms 1–59, 60–150.* 2 vols. Minneapolis: Augsburg, 1988, 1993.

Limburg, James. *Psalms.* Louisville: Westminster John Knox, 2000.

Mays, James Luther. *Psalms.* Interpretation Series. Louisville: Westminster John Knox, 1994.

McCann, J. Clinton, Jr. *1 & 2 Maccabees, Job, Psalms.* New Interpreter's Bible, 4. Leander Keck, gen. ed. Nashville: Abingdon Press, 1996.

NIV Study Bible. Zondervan, 2002. With notes by John Stek.

Psalms. Word Biblical Commentary, 19-21. Waco, TX: Word, 1983. Volumes by Peter C. Craigie, Marvin E. Tate, Leslie C. Allen.

Terrien, Samuel. *The Psalms: Strophic Structure and Theological Commentary.* Grand Rapids: Eerdmans, 2003.

Weiser, Artur. *The Psalms: A Commentary.* Trans. Herbert Hartwell. London: SCM Press, 1971.

C. Bible Study Curriculum for Congregational and Small Group Use

The following are a modest sampling of the hundreds of available curriculum materials for general education purposes within congregations. These volumes assume no scholarly background.

Futato, Mark D. *Joy Comes in the Morning: Psalms for All Seasons.* Phillipsburg, NJ: Presbyterian and Reformed Publishing, 2004.

————. *Transformed by Praise: The Purpose and Message of the Psalms.* Phillipsburg, NJ: Presbyterian and Reformed Publishing, 2002.

Griggs, Donald L. *Passion, Promise, and Praise: Discovering the Psalms.* The Kerygma Program, 1993.

Kaiser, Walter. *Psalms: Heart to Heart with God.* Grand Rapids: Zondervan, 1995.

Peterson, Eugene. *A Long Obedience in the Same Direction.* Downers Grove, IL: InterVarsity Press, 1996.

Rudie, Carol Veldman. *Discover God in the Psalms.* Grand Rapids: CRC Publications, 2000.

Smit, Harvey A. *Psalms: Speaking Honestly with God.* 2 vols. Grand Rapids: CRC Publications, 2002.

Vander Ark, Daniel. *Honest to God: A Study of the Psalms.* Grand Rapids: Bible Cross-roads/CRC Publications, 1988.

Acknowledgments

It is a great privilege to work at a college and seminary that both encourage academic excellence and are deeply committed to the life of the church. Given the context of this vibrant community, I have many people to thank for contributing to this work, and I already regret that I may have inadvertently missed some. I am particularly grateful

> to Carl J. Bosma for first introducing me to the joys of studying the Psalms;
>
> to Emily R. Brink, John Hamersma, Bert Polman, Calvin Seerveld, Howard Slenk, Calvin Stapert, and John Stek — who each for several decades have testified to the value of the Psalms in their teaching and scholarship;
>
> to Nathan Bierma, Joyce Borger, Carl J. Bosma, Emily R. Brink, Paul Detterman, Michael Hawn, Scott Hoezee, Rolf Jacobsen, Rachel Klompmaker, Bert Polman, Debra Rienstra, Ron Rienstra, Lester Ruth, Paul Ryan, Greg Scheer, Ed Seely, Betsy Steele Halstead, Carrie Steenwyk, Paul Westermeyer, and Joyce Zimmerman — for comments on earlier drafts of this paper;
>
> to Joy Berg, Lee Couch, Mimi Farra, Karin Gargone, Dan Grimminger, Sally Hart, Joe Herl, Heather Josselyn-Cranson, Janet Loman, David Music, Bert Polman, Michael Silhavy, LuAnn Steiner, Adam Tice, Robin Wallace, and Ester Widiasih — all participants in the summer

2006 Calvin College faculty seminar on teaching hymnology — for their insightful comments;

to Matt Gritter, Katie Ritsema, and especially to Carrie Steenwyk for research assistance;

to Carl J. Bosma, Norma de Waal Malefyt, and Howard Vanderwell, who developed an integrated series of Lenten services based on the Psalms during the completion of this book (see www.calvin.edu/worship/psalms);

to Walter Brueggemann, Stephen Breck Reid, Ellen Davis, Clinton McCann, and Patrick Miller, who each presented lectures on the Psalms at Calvin College or Calvin Theological Seminary during the past several years, and provided a wonderful window not only to recent scholarship on the Psalms, but to the Psalms themselves;

to Emily Brink, Cindy de Jong, Norma de Waal Malefyt, Elizabeth Holmlund, Brooks Kuykendall, Robert Nordling, Jodi MacLean, and Laura Smit, who led the Calvin College community in preparing a Psalm vigil (with settings of all 150 Psalms over an eight-hour period on one beautiful fall evening) during the time in which this book was being completed;

to Mary Hulst, Duane Kelderman, Neal Plantinga, Jack Roeda, Fleming Rutledge, Clay Schmit, Laura Smit, Leonard Vander Zee, and John L. Witvliet, who preached sermons on the Psalms in ways that changed my thinking and challenged my faith; to Jimmie Abbington, Anton Armstrong, Randy Engle, John Ferguson, David Fuentes, Marty Haugen, Roy Hopp, Jorge Lockward, Merle Mustert, Joel Navarro, Don Saliers, Charsie Sawyer, Pearl Shangkuan, Greg Scheer, and Marcia Van Oyen, who once composed or led the singing of a Psalm in worship in a way that helped me see new possibilities.

to Sonja Arevalo, Fiona Baker, Cynthia DeBoer, Nathan Bierma, Joyce Borger, Emily Brink, Emily Cooper, Kent DeYoung, Norma de Waal Malefyt, Betty Grit, Bert Polman, Paul Ryan, Greg Scheer, Ed Seely, Kathy Smith, Carrie Steenwyk, Connie Van Groningen, Howard Vanderwell, Kristen Verhulst, and Anne Zaki — for daily encouragement in our work together;

to Calvin Brondyke, Matt Gritter, Kent Hendricks, Courtney Hexham,

Brenda Janssen, Rachel Klompmaker, Joanna Kooyenga, Steven Koster, Asher Mains, Bethany Meyer, Becky Ochsner, and Katie Ritsema, who work at CICW as student assistants, but also do a lot of good teaching through perceptive questions;

to Craig Dykstra and the Lilly Endowment for their encouragement and financial support, without which this volume would not have been possible;

to Roger Van Harn for commissioning this work in conjunction with the *Eerdmans Lectionary Commentary;*

to Charlotte for her loving encouragement, partnership, and support in every aspect of daily life;

and to Sheila Grace, Madeline, Katherine, and Luke, to whom this book is dedicated, for daily demonstrating the vibrancy of life that is God's gift to us. May they come to cherish the Psalms as much as their great-grandparents did.

Permissions

pp. 3-4   Basil the Great, *Homilia in psalmum i, 2, Patrologiae cursus completus, series graeca*, ed. J. P. Migne, vol. 29 (Paris, 1857-1866), col. 209-212; trans. in James McKinnon, ed., *Music in Early Christian Literature* (New York: Cambridge University Press, 1987), p. 65. Copyright © 1987 Cambridge University Press. Reprinted with the permission of Cambridge University Press.

pp. 4-6   Ambrose, *Explanatio psalmi i, 7, 9*; in *Patrologiae cursus completus, series latina*, ed. J. P. Migne, vol. 14 (Paris, 1844-1864), col. 923-925; trans. in James McKinnon, ed., *Music in Early Christian Literature* (New York: Cambridge University Press, 1987), p. 126. Copyright © 1987 Cambridge University Press. Reprinted with the permission of Cambridge University Press.

pp. 6-7   John Chrysostom, *In psalmum xli, 1-2*, in *Patrologiae cursus completus, series graeca*, ed. J. P. Migne, vol. 55 (Paris, 1857-1866), col. 157-158; trans. in James McKinnon, ed., *Music in Early Christian Literature* (New York: Cambridge University Press, 1987), pp. 80-81. Copyright © 1987 Cambridge University Press. Reprinted with the permission of Cambridge University Press.

pp. 7-8   Athanasius, *St. Athanasius on the Incarnation: The Treatise* De Incarnatione Verbi Dei, trans. and ed. a Religious of C.S.M.V., rev. ed. (Crestwood, NY: St. Vladimir's Orthodox Theological Seminary, 1953-1978), pp. 103, 105-6. Copyright © 1953/1978 St. Vladimir's Seminary. Reprinted by permission of St. Vladimir's Seminary Press, 575 Scarsdale Rd., Crestwood, NY 10707-1699. 800/204-2665

Index of Names

Index of Subjects

Adoration, 25, 140

Advent, 54, 55, 102, 105

African American worship, 13, 33, 107, 108

Anglican chant, 96, 98-99, 102, 150

Antiphons, 56, 62, 91, 94, 97, 99, 101, 102, 103, 105, 106

Antithetical parallelism, 83

Apostolic Constitutions, 133

Ascension, 55

Ascent, 71

Ash Wednesday, 54

Baptism (or baptismal), 22, 23, 53, 56, 60, 133, 146

Benediction, 17, 56, 68, 73, 84, 140

Biblical canticles, 14, 123

Blues, 119

Cadence, 27, 63, 75, 77, 82, 83, 94

Calligraphy, 124-25

Canonical order, 51-52

Cantillation, 100

CCLI, 118

Chant, xiii, xvii, 85, 94, 96-101, 112, 118, 125, 127, 128, 136

Charismatic worship, xvi, xviii, 102, 117

Children, 3, 6, 11, 106, 124, 126-27, 128, 129

Choral reading, 74, 80, 81, 82, 85, 87-90, 117, 129

Christian year, 22, 52-55

Christmas, 24, 54

Christological framing, 74-75

Collect, 24, 75-76, 135

Common meter, 110

Communal speech/prayer, 26, 28, 34, 51, 52, 53, 65, 70, 76, 87, 135

Communion (Lord's Supper), 47, 53, 55

Confession, 25, 43, 53, 55, 68, 78, 121-22

Contemplation, 16, 72-74

Contemporary worship, xvii, 60, 86, 116-20

Country music, 118

Covenant, 11, 16, 21, 30, 58, 71

Daily prayer, xviii, 61, 80, 91

Dialogic structure (or dialogue), 16, 81

Early church, 23, 48, 53

Easter, 54, 105

Emerging worship, xvi, xvii, 116-20

English Psalmody, 98, 110

Enthronement Psalms, 14, 71

Epiphany, 54

Eucharist, 22, 23, 104

Evangelism, 61, 117

Extemporaneous prayers, 84, 120-23

Folk music, xiii, 47, 86, 102, 103, 104, 105, 106, 116-19

Gelineau Psalmody, 99-100, 106
Genevan Psalmody, 107, 110, 111, 114
Gloria Patri, 76
Good Friday, 53, 54
Grail Psalter, 66, 99, 100

Hallel Psalms, 54
Historical Psalms, 20, 70
Historical recitation, 17
Homiletical criteria. *See* Preaching
Hospitality, 132-34, 146
Hymns of praise, 26, 53, 71
Hymn Society in the United States and Canada, 130

Iambic meter, 108-9
Image/imagery, 5, 31, 32, 33, 35, 47, 50, 59-60, 63, 71, 75, 77, 101, 108, 117, 118, 124
Imprecatory Psalms, 73, 74
Improvised prayer, 120-23
Intercession, 25, 29, 53, 72-73
Intergenerational worship, 126-27
Iona Community, 108, 122
I-Psalms, 26

Jazz music, 29, 47, 98, 102, 103, 116, 118
Justice, xviii, 18, 29, 30, 32, 61

Lament, 14, 20, 23, 25, 26, 28, 31, 32, 34, 35, 47, 49, 50, 51, 55, 57, 68, 69, 70, 77, 79, 80-81, 86, 91, 92, 140
Lectionary, xiii, xvi, xvii, 33, 45, 46, 51, 52-56, 61, 68, 103, 104, 105, 126, 131
Lent, 54, 105
Liturgical criteria, 49
Liturgical Movement, The, 13
Liturgical placement, 48, 67-68
Liturgical prayer, 14, 23, 26, 28, 29, 32, 33, 35, 63, 72
Liturgical renewal, 51
Long meter, 109
Lord's Supper, xviii, 55, 68, 111, 133, 146

Maundy Thursday, 54
Messianic Psalms, 71, 74
Metaphor, 16, 17, 18, 23, 28, 32, 33, 34, 47, 59-60, 83, 117
Meter, 108-10
Metrical Psalmody, xvi, 31, 56, 68, 75, 85, 92, 93, 94, 97, 106-14, 117-18, 119, 125, 129
Monastic worship, xvii, 13, 51, 69, 91, 92
Mysticism, 21

Names for God, 18, 20, 23
Narrative, 21, 22, 23, 53, 58-60, 72

Pace, 77, 78, 82, 86, 91-92, 94, 97
Palm Sunday, 54
Parallelism, 50, 78, 82-83, 96, 108
Paraphrase, 47, 62-67, 101, 113, 114, 120-23, 143
Pastoral care, 46, 48, 61-62, 143
Pastoral criteria, xiv, 49, 61-62, 116-17
Pentecost, 55
Pilgrim Psalms, 71
Plainchant, 100-101
Poetic lines, 24, 33, 34, 50, 62-63, 66, 81-82, 83, 86, 87, 91, 92, 96, 110
Pointed text, 96-97, 98, 101
Praise and Worship, 118-19
Prayer book, 13, 31, 46, 56, 59, 67, 72, 132, 138-39, 140-41
Prayer of Thanksgiving, 22, 25
Preaching, xiv, xv, 17, 26, 30, 31, 33, 45, 49, 56-60, 68, 72-74, 79, 83, 84, 87, 116, 143, 146-47
Psalm classification, 93
Psalm prayers, 75
Psalm types, 70-71

Reformation, 37
Refrains, 60, 74, 92-93, 95, 100, 101-6, 115, 123, 127
Responsive readings, 15, 82, 85, 91-93, 101-2, 122
Responsorial Psalmody, xvii, 45, 74, 85, 91-

Index of Psalms